* * * * * * * * * * * * * * * * * * *

Starting
Kids
Off
Right

* * * * * * * * * * * * * * * * * * *

How to Raise
Confident Children
Who Can Make Friends
and Build Healthy
Relationships

* * * * * * * * * * * * * *

Starting Kids Off Right

* * * * * * * * * * * *

Stephen Nowicki Jr., Ph.D.
Marshall P. Duke, Ph.D.
Amy Van Buren, Ph.D.

PEACHTREE
ATLANTA

Published by
PEACHTREE PUBLISHERS
1700 Chattahoochee Avenue
Atlanta, Georgia 30318-2112

www.peachtree-online.com

Text © 2008 by Stephen Nowicki Jr., Ph.D., Marshall P. Duke, Ph.D., and Amy Van Buren, Ph.D.

Book design by Regina Dalton Fischel
Composition by Robin Sherman

Printed in the United States of America
10 9 8 7 6 5 4 3 2 1
First Edition

Cataloging-in-Publication Data is available from the Library of Congress

ISBN 13: 978-1-56145-447-1
ISBN 10: 1-56145-447-8

For Sharon, Lee, Brandon, Alex, Jakey, Emma, Noah, Gabrielle,
Rachel, Shira, Jon, Susan, Lila, Andy, Jenny, Hannah, Soren, and Nicholas

TABLE OF CONTENTS

CHAPTER V

THE JUVENILE STAGE (FIVE TO TEN YEARS) 131

INTRODUCTION

Beyond hearing that a child is doing well in school, few things make a parent's heart leap for joy more than hearing that a child "has friends." There is something affirming about learning that offspring are liked by others their age. We are, of course, proud of them and pleased for them. But these are not the only reasons. Hearing that our children are liked may also recall our own childhood memories. We remember the fun of being around other children whom we called friends, and we remember the awful feeling of being rejected or left out or not counted among a friendship group. Whether we like it or not, having friends—being in relationships with others—is important for our children's happiness. As parents or caregivers, we recognize that the skills needed to make friends originate during the early years of a child's life. It will be largely through our love and guidance that these skills are formed and nurtured.

Professionals who observe children find a variety of friendship and relational patterns. Some kids seem to make friends easily; others have a little more difficulty, but eventually do okay; while a smaller number of children struggle to make and keep friends and may even end up with no friends at all. Probably some parents believe children either have it or don't have it when it comes to making friends. To be sure, there are some children who seem to have natural interpersonal skills. However, the ability to make friends is just that—an ability—and one that takes roughly the first five years of life to develop. Some people are really good at this skill, some are fair, and others are poor at it. And because it is a skill, it can be taught, learned, practiced, and mastered. This is what this book is all about—the whys and hows of relationship building in kids up to the age of twelve.

As psychologists interested in relationships, we have spent decades studying the mechanisms through which people interact. In two previous books on this subject—*Helping the Child Who Doesn't Fit In* and *Teaching Your Child the Language of Social Success*—we focused on nonverbal language and the ways in which mastery of facial expressions, gestures, postures, personal space, voice tones, and the like help children become more effective interpersonally. Here, in this book, we broaden our scope to include more about relationships and how they develop. Our goal is to help parents and teachers of children to become relationship experts, to better understand the interpersonal worlds of the children in their care so they can guide them to increasingly richer and better relationships.

We have organized the book by developmental levels so that you, after reading the introductory material that describes how relationships work, can move more quickly to the section appropriate to the age group that concerns you. We tried to minimize psychological jargon and we included essential information from our own and others' research. Our goal is to help you become successful relationship teachers.

Starting Kids Off Right is composed of five chapters. The first chapter explains what we mean by "relationship" and describes how relationships work. The second chapter discusses the role that nonverbal communication and other communication skills play in forming relationships. The remaining three chapters are in-depth examinations of each of the three developmental time periods—from the infant and toddler years when most relationship learning is with adults through the early school years when the major relationship learning takes place with peers.

We distinguish three distinct developmental time periods:

1) **infant** (birth to around two years);

2) **child** (from around two to four or five years of age); and

3) **juvenile** (from about four or five to around nine or ten years of age).

We also consider what we call the ***chum*** relationship of pre-adolescence (from around ten to twelve years of age). You can concentrate your reading on the time period that is of most interest to you, but keep in mind that the skills learned in the early periods provide the foundation for later development.

CHAPTER I

WHAT ARE RELATIONSHIPS AND HOW DO THEY WORK?

✳

Sullivan's theory of human relationships

The four phases of a relationship

My daughter Ida is six months old. I'm over being scared of having a baby, but I don't know what I should be doing with her to help her to be happy...to get her ready for all that's ahead of her.

✻

Neha has just started preschool and I'm so nervous for her. I watched her the other day and all she does is stand in the corner and play with a doll. She doesn't talk to any of the other children. I don't want to force her to do something she doesn't want to do, but is she okay?

✻

I don't know if it is right or not but I'm concerned about Barney. Every time he scores a basket in a game, he does this trash talking and acts like he is big stuff. I see other kids doing that as well, but I wonder if I should come down hard on him. I'm afraid his being so cocky will stop him from having friends. And boy, what a poor loser! You'd think the world was coming to an end. Is that right? Should he be that upset?

✻

Janice and Tomika are like Siamese twins joined at the hip. They go everywhere together. Yesterday, when Tomika came home it wasn't two minutes before she was on the phone to Janice about something. I'm worried about them spending so much time together. Don't they need to have other friends?

Problems, problems, problems! So many of the important and troubling problems children have involve relating to others. As parents, one of our constant concerns is helping our children learn how to get along with others. This book provides ways to address relationship difficulties.

Watch elementary children at recess. See how they separate into groups of boys and girls. Many of the girls are most likely talking intently with one another in groups of two or three or playing catch or jumping rope. Most of the boys are probably interacting in larger groups, playing games with rules that have winners and losers, like soccer, kick ball, or football. But you may also see some children who do not interact with the others: Girls who stand alone, hands folded, looking down with no one to talk to. Boys who are on the periphery of the game, pawing the ground nervously because they were not chosen by either side and thus cannot play. Such children don't want to be alone, but that's where they've ended up.

Being excluded can happen much earlier than elementary school. Observe a preschool class. Children mill around, participating in what seems, at first, to be random and chaotic activities. Some run around, some sit, and some just look around the room. In time, however, this seeming chaos reveals itself as purposeful play. Most children arrange themselves around types of playthings like the sandbox or around kinds of activities such as playing cars. They grab trucks and roll them on the ground, making noises like roaring engines, engaging the interest of other children. They create sand castles. They sit side by side looking at books. But even at this young age, you can see children who do not seem to be connected to others. They are at the party, but outside of the festivities. They not only don't know how to get in, they may not even know to knock on the door.

What's a parent to do?

Our answer: Become more knowledgeable about relationships so that you can respond effectively to guide and support the ever-changing, continuously occurring interpersonal interactions your children will experience throughout their young lives. We begin with some basic ideas about the way relationships operate. There are, of course, many studies of how people learn to interact with one another, but we have found the ideas of Harry Stack Sullivan to be most helpful in explaining how young children learn to relate to others.

Sullivan's theory of human relationships

Harry Stack Sullivan was what is known as an interpersonal psychiatrist. Rather than focusing on what goes on inside individual people as his Freudian predecessors and colleagues were doing, Sullivan believed that the most important things in life go on between people. His special contribution was helping us become aware that one of the worst psychological pains humans experience is loneliness—the feeling that we are not connected to others and that we are helpless to change the situation. We need to emphasize here that *choosing* to be alone is not the sort of pain that Sullivan meant; quiet moments alone can be welcomed. What concerned Sullivan was involuntary solitude—being alone and wishing not to be, but having no way to remedy the situation. The antidotes for loneliness are simple and straightforward— interpersonal contact, connections with others, relationships.

Sullivan saw relationships as essential to a life filled with satisfactions and free of unnecessary psychological pain. Relationships were so important to him that he generated a theory of social development based on them, and he saw interpersonal relationships with teachers, counselors, and psychotherapists as the sources of help for people who had gone so far into loneliness that they were in need of special guidance to recover from it.

Knowledge of Sullivan's theory of interpersonal development is a first step in understanding the specific relationship needs of children at various ages. He described several stages of life, each energized by a drive toward richer and more complex relationships and distinguished by a different, more mature manner of interacting with others.

FIRST STAGE: INFANCY (BIRTH TO TWO YEARS)

When children are born there is no such thing as interpersonal, there is only personal. At birth, despite being physically separated from their mothers, infants are not yet psychologically separated from them. Newborns have not yet differentiated between themselves and their primary caregivers (who most often are their mothers). This psychological fusion between mothers and their children can produce a variety of outcomes.

First, infants tend to feel what their mothers feel. This is shown nicely in the following interaction between a calm mother and a distressed infant in need of soothing.

ETHAN

✳ ✳ ✳

Four-month-old Ethan is having a difficult time falling asleep. He is fussing and has begun to cry. His mother knows he is tired and ready to sleep and has given him some time to settle down, but that is not happening. She goes over to the crib, bends over, and says in a soothing voice, "Ethan, you're just having a rough time of it, aren't you?"

She rubs his back while she sings the lullaby that she remembers from her own childhood. It takes a while but the steady, calm hand motions and the gentle singing voice calm Ethan down and soon he is sound asleep.

Ethan, like most infants his age, can feel what his mother is feeling. His mother has communicated her calmness through her touch and her voice, and he has responded by calming down. Through this special kind of communication between mothers and their children, infants soon learn how to pick up cues of calmness (or anxiety) not only from the primary caregiver but from others with whom they interact.

Sullivan suggests that the interpersonal development of infants begins when children have a budding realization that mother (or another caregiver) does not, in fact, always know what is going on in their minds and that, in fact, they actually are separate from their parents. At this point, the fusion relationship fades and psychological separation leads infants to develop an attachment relationship with their mothers (and sometimes with fathers or other caregivers), through which they eventually will learn how to interact with others. As children become more aware of their separation, they learn ways of staying connected to their sources of physical and psychological support. This is where learning to communicate comes in.

For the early infant, the communication patterns are relatively simple: cry if you want something, and hope that mom or dad will figure out what that something is. Happily, at this time there are only a few possibilities, so parents can function pretty well within this primitive level of information and interaction. As the child's needs become more complex, however, it becomes necessary for the child and the parents to develop more sophisticated forms of communication, first nonverbally and then within two years, verbally. It is at this point that we see the beginnings of sophisticated signals like facial expressions (e.g., turning away the mouth when offered baby food spinach, but smiling and opening wide for baby food chocolate pudding), gestures, vocalizations (coos and grunts), and then later, real words! When words appear, according to Sullivan, the child is ready to move into the next stage of social development, childhood.

Second Stage: Childhood (Two to Four or Five Years)

Heather Jane

* * *

Grandma and Grandpa are having lunch with their granddaughter Heather Jane, who is visiting with her mother, June. Although there is much smiling and fun, things are not going well. Heather Jane keeps saying that she wants "buttoo." Grandma and Grandpa have no idea what that means, and they are becoming frustrated. Luckily June is in the other room and explains that buttoo is Heather Jane's word for peanut butter. Once this is cleared up, they are able to give Heather Jane what she is asking for, and lunchtime is much more pleasant for everyone.

The real words that begin to appear in most two-year-olds' vocabulary are typically words that work within the special relationships among kids and their immediate family. Mom and Dad know that "buttoo" means peanut butter or "getti" means spaghetti, and they all get along pretty well. However, there is a big difference between communicating to people in a limited family universe and communicating to people in the world at large. It is the task of the parent to teach the child a system of communication that will allow him to relate effectively outside of his family. This process requires a few years, typically from ages two through five, and is accomplished largely through refined and enriched experiences guided by the attachment relationship with his mother.

During this childhood stage of social development, language shaping develops verbally and nonverbally. Parents are typically torn about what to teach during this time. On the one hand, they love the cute baby talk and vocalizations and treasure the special funny words and goofy facial expressions that they and their child share with one another. But they are also aware that the special words and nonverbal communications cannot be used outside the family circle. Thus, parents begin to carefully "shape" their child's verbal language by repeating the correct pronunciations of various words, restating sentences with proper grammar, and reducing their children's (and their) dependence on "baby talk." They refine their child's nonverbal expressions by using more subtle facial expressions. Over time, early word forms drop away, more universal words appear more frequently, and facial expressions, tones of voice, and gestures become more sophisticated.

As part of the teaching enterprise implicit in the attachment relationship, parents select other children with whom their child is going to interact, initiating play dates and sleepovers. Parents typically structure these interactions by deciding what the children are going to do, where they're going to do it, and for how long. They are usually present to orchestrate and choreograph the activities. In this way, children learn to interact with others of their same age—a crucial skill for the next developmental stage.

While maintaining control of their young children's interactions, parents also leave children some room to relate with others on their own. It takes time and experience for children to develop the social awareness or knowledge to do things like wait their turn or share their toys or food. An arranged interaction presents an opportunity for parents to teach their children what's okay and what's not okay about the way they interact with another person.

Familiarity—parents know the child who plays with their child and know the parents of that child—makes an ideal teaching and learning situation. Moms and dads have this degree of control over who their children's playmates (or potential friends) are only during the childhood stage. Since this level of control (and sense of security) is short-lived, parents need to take every opportunity to socialize their child at this stage. When children begin full-time school, they will be in social situations with relative strangers and without parental supervision.

THIRD STAGE: JUVENILE ERA (ABOUT FIVE TO TEN YEARS)

When a child begins school, she enters what Sullivan termed the juvenile stage. When Sullivan was writing, most children didn't start school until kindergarten at age five and didn't begin full-day school until age six. But even though children start preschool earlier today, Sullivan's ideas still hold. Unlike in the play dates and sleepovers of childhood, during the preschool years children meet, play with, and establish relationships with other children who are strangers to them and their parents. But they do this under the watchful eyes of teachers and aides. In many cases, the parents have carefully chosen the schools. Preschool may be seen as a sort of higher order play date when, rather than being exposed to a single specific child that the parents select, a child is put with a larger number of a particular type of child (one whose parents also feel that this particular preschool is a good one). We can look at the preschool years as a bridge from the child stage to the juvenile stage.

In first grade, when children begin formal schooling, the juvenile era really begins. Now, the child is placed in a class and may be assigned a seat according to alphabetical order by last name or scores on some objective test, not on the basis of making friendships work out. Studies show, by the way, that children who are seated alphabetically in school tend to establish closest friendships with other people whose names begin with letters within two or three letters of theirs in the alphabet. Proximity turns out to be one of the most powerful predictors of friendships.

In the juvenile era, children's social relationships are qualitatively different from how they were in infancy and childhood. For the first time in their young lives children are attempting to form relationships as an equal instead of following the direction of adults. More than ever before, they must rely on their own devices and decisions and behaviors when relating to others. Some children never successfully make this transition and remain comfortable only in situations where adults control them and the social setting. To make this transition to a different type of social situation, children must depend on what they've learned during their attachment relationships.

Most often, juvenile era friends are members of the same sex, and they generally play in groups (larger groups for boys than for girls). Though elementary school age children are learning to make same-gender friends on their own, social learning and interaction still takes place in the presence of adults, usually teachers. The mark of the juvenile era is interpersonal experimenting. Possible friendships appear, are tried out, and nearly always fade away or end quickly.

Parenting a juvenile era child involves continuing efforts to extend selected interactions that fit the play-date pattern to activities like scouts, ballet lessons, karate, baseball, basketball, soccer, and other group sports. Understandably, parents of children in elementary school are torn between allowing their children increasing independence in their friendships and simultaneously trying to control (as much as possible) the pool of potential good friends.

LATER STAGES OF DEVELOPMENT
(ABOUT NINE TO EARLY ADOLESCENCE)

Preadolescence is a time of transition between the many same-sex friendships of childhood and the opposite-sex relationships of adolescence. Somewhere between the ages of nine and twelve, most children will have opportunities to form strong, same-sex close friendships with other kids their age in which they can explore and resolve issues of trust and caring that will carry over into adolescence. Sullivan described this special friend as a "chum" or a "best-best friend."

Chums pair off from the larger social group and spend large amounts of time communicating with one another by any means available to them (in person, by phone, or by e-mail). Any topic is fair game for these best friends, but making sense of their own and others' relationships is the major topic. Parents, teachers, and other adults may be discussed, but most of the time is devoted to discussing their peers and their hairstyles, clothing, likes and dislikes. What is important about these discussions is that both members of the pair, or "chum dyad," trust what the other person says. Through what Sullivan called **consensual validation**, chums provide one another not only with valuable information about social interactions and social behavior but also with feedback about what the other person is doing right and wrong in these situations.

Parents often seem to be left out of their children's friendships at this stage, but parents need to be aware of the importance of chum relationships and do as much as they can to encourage their development.

When children begin to have sexual feelings and thoughts (and occasionally even participate in sexual activities), they leave preadolescence and enter early and middle adolescence, developmental stages that are beyond the scope of this book. Sullivan believed, as do we, that the success of social experiences in adolescence is based upon how much was learned about interactions and relationships during the four earlier stages. A chum relationship could not develop fully unless the child has learned the fundamentals of peer friendships that originate in the juvenile era. In turn, the peer friendships of the juvenile era would not be possible without the orchestrated learning that took place in childhood. Play dates of childhood could never be successful unless infants were able to form secure attachment relationships through which they learn basic communication skills.

The four phases of a relationship

Now that we have traced the growth of the increasingly complex relationship interactions that characterize children's development and require ever-increasing interpersonal skills to accomplish, we want to turn our discussion to the relationship process itself. How do relationships get going, and what makes some work out and others fail?

We identify four phases within a relationship: choice, beginning, deepening, and ending. To move successfully from one phase to the next requires numerous skills, both verbal and non-verbal, that must be learned.

The Choice Phase

Jimmy

✳ ✳ ✳

The playground is filled with children on the first day of school. Seven-year-old Jimmy steps down from the school bus and looks at the moving mass of children in front of him. He has thirty minutes before classes begin. Jimmy is new to this school and wants to find someone to play with. But how? Over to the left are three boys playing catch; one boy looks up from chasing a ball and smiles. Jimmy notices he is wearing a Green Bay Packers hat. Green Bay is Jimmy's favorite team. That makes up his mind. "I'm going to ask those guys if I can play with them," he says to himself and he begins to walk toward the boy who smiled.

Every day we face relationship choices. If you are lost and need to ask for directions, how do you decide whom to ask? This quandary is similar to what children face when attempting to relate to others.

Jimmy, new to a school, enters a playground filled with other children and looks around for someone to play with. He is exercising his newfound independence to choose same-age, same-sex playmates. Younger children rarely have control over choosing playmates, but even infants and toddlers have preferences regarding the peers they like and the ones they do not like. During the juvenile and preadolescent stages, decisions about the choice of playmates falls more and more under the control of children and becomes increasingly important because their decisions determine the group of children with whom they will be identified.

All relationships begin with a choice, and a bad choice can doom any relationship before it begins. In spite of their importance, most choices are made quickly on the basis of very subtle and limited information that is usually nonverbal. Researchers have found that adults and children will take about seven seconds to decide with whom they will choose to begin a relationship. In such a brief amount of time, the information can only come from nonverbal cues such as posture, dress, and facial expressions. Children who lack nonverbal skills are at a particular disadvantage in forming a relationship, especially at the choice phase.

Ideally, as parents of younger children choose playmates for their sons and daughters, they also explain to children how and why they are making these decisions. When parents are clear about their criteria for choosing, their children are better prepared to make choices on their own when the time comes. For example, a child could be told that Demetrius is going to be asked over to play because he "listens, is polite, shares with others, and doesn't hit others when he gets angry." Not only does such information help children understand their parents' decisions, but it also underlines what they are expecting from their own children.

THE BEGINNING PHASE

JIMMY

✳ ✳ ✳

Jimmy walks toward the three boys playing ball. He waits until there's a lull in the activity. "Hi, I'm Jimmy," he says with a smile. "Can I play?" He waits again until the other boys introduce themselves. When they are finished he says, "I'm a Packer Backer, too. I've got a Packers hat at home. I'll wear it tomorrow."

The boy with the Packers hat says, "Yeah, there's a few of us good guys here. Remember when they won that game where it was about a million degrees below zero?" Jimmy excitedly comments about how the field was like ice, and soon there are four boys playing.

Choosing a person with whom to initiate a relationship (an important ability in itself) requires one set of skills. A second set of skills comes into play during the next phase, called the beginning. How do you begin relating to someone, and how do you respond to someone who has begun to relate to you? Beginning skills are learned throughout all stages of social development and become more important as children move into juvenile and preadolescence stages. Beginnings are comparatively easy for two children whose moms have set up everything, including what the children will be doing. It is a much harder task for two eleven-year-olds who meet at a party to which they were invited by a mutual friend. Children with a knack for beginning relationships can get things going easily, while those who lack these skills will suffer and may be left out in the cold.

But there is help for those who have trouble with beginnings. While our culture doesn't provide much guidance with choosing, deepening, or ending a relationship, it does give us some advice for what to do during the beginning phase. Parents can teach their children a specific code of rules and conduct called "etiquette" or "manners." It is easy to see that Jimmy has already learned the basics. He acted as most adults do to begin a relationship. As he approached other children he waited for a break in their activities so that he wouldn't intrude, then he smiled and introduced himself, said something amounting to small talk about the Packers, and then asked if he could play. We believe that most children's social difficulties in beginning relationships occur because they did not learn about etiquette and manners from parents and teachers.

THE DEEPENING PHASE

EILEEN AND HANNAH

✳ ✳ ✳

Eileen, a fourth-grader, comes huffing and puffing through the front door. "Mom," she calls, "I'm home. What a day I had at school. Hannah was wearing the same dress as Mary Ellen and neither one knew it until they got to math. Then I lost my purse, but Hannah found it for me before I got too panicked. I got an A on my paper, the one Hannah helped me with...and she got an A on her paper, the one I helped her with. Can I have a cookie? I've got to call Hannah and see what she thinks of tomorrow's assignment. See you later, Mom."

Eileen and Hannah have a deepening relationship. Knowing how to deepen relationships becomes more important as we move from childhood into juvenile and preadolescent stages. A deep relationship for a three-year-old or a seven-year-old is much different from the close relationship with a best friend or chum at age eleven. Deepening occurs when children go beyond the beginning of a relationship and show preference for and trust in someone for a significant amount of time. For younger children, attaining attachment relationships with parents, grandparents, or other adults reflects proper deepening for this stage of development. But it would be unlikely if not impossible for children in infancy or childhood to achieve relationships with peers anywhere near as deep as what we would expect from juvenile and pre-adolescent kids like Hannah and Eileen.

During the childhood stage, when children are between eighteen months and four or five years old, they often have many acquaintances but very few true friends (in a true friendship they would put others' needs consistently ahead of their own). There is nothing wrong with this. They are not developmentally ready—emotionally or cognitively—to relate at a more mature level. It is important for parents to understand that there are limits to younger children's abilities to deepen a relationship and relate to others in a consistent, trustworthy fashion. Parents need to model how to deepen a relationship by responding to the inconsistent behaviors of their children in consistent and trustworthy ways, both verbally and nonverbally. Too often infants and children pull adults to their level of interaction, rather than vice versa. How many times have you found yourself in this argument with your five-year-old?

"You have to go to bed now!"

"No, I won't!"

"Yes, you will!"

"No, no, no!"

"Yes, yes, yes."

We could go on, but you know how it goes.

Relationship deepening becomes more intense and meaningful in late childhood and preadolescence as children develop best friends or chums. Sullivan believed the development of a best-friend relationship marks the first time in a child's life when he truly puts the others' wishes, desires, and needs ahead of his own. Sullivan further suggests that this is the first time children truly can love! In fact, Sullivan believed that this new capacity to love helps children think about and love their parents in a more mature way. We're not sure we would go that far, but we do agree that learning how to deepen a relationship is crucial to becoming complete and happy adults.

The verbal and nonverbal communication skills used in successful choice and beginning phases are different from those needed for deepening. Deepening calls for a higher level of openness and honesty and a greater commitment of time and effort. Recall that, by definition, the chum relationship is the deepest relationship of childhood. It serves as a template for future close adolescent and adult relationships. (Don't expect young children's relationships to be of comparable intensity to a chumship. Just enjoy them where they are.)

THE ENDING PHASE

GINA AND ILANA

✳ ✳ ✳

It is the last day of school for ten-year-old Gina and Ilana. The two girls sat next to each other during class for the whole school year because their last names both begin with M. On the whole, they get along fairly well; their only real argument was about which kind of shoes are cuter. While not "best friends," they like each other and are sad that they probably won't see much of each other over the summer. As they look over old papers, throwing most of them away, they talk about fun things that happened over the academic year. When their desks have passed their teacher's inspection and it is time to leave, they both sheepishly produce little presents for each other. They wish each other a fun summer and say they will look for one another when they start back to school in the fall.

Just like every day must end, so must every relationship. We might not like it, but we need to make the best of it. A new relationship with the person might start again later, but only after the old relationship has ended. When we have difficulty successfully ending relationships, the unended relationships stay with us, sapping the energy and strength we need to begin other new relationships successfully.

Children, especially young children, easily and frequently connect and disconnect with other kids all the time. Young children form brief relationships with peers their parents know, or they may play on a sports team for a time with groups of children they never see again after the big game and party at the end of the season. They start up relationships in swimming pools and on playgrounds and while on vacations, see these other children a few times, and then may never see them again. A big difference between endings for children and adults is that, more often than not, younger kids don't have much to say about them. However, as children grow older, endings become more important because their relationships become more serious and complex. Every year students begin school-based relationships that continue until the last day of school, when they end.

How to handle endings is an important and difficult—and often neglected—relationship skill. Gina and Ilana must have observed or been taught that it is an important ritual to give small presents to one another when saying good-bye to a friend. Without such learning children may overlook or "forget" to acknowledge the importance of their friendships. Since most endings in the infant and childhood stages are controlled by parents, we hope parents will spend some time teaching their children how to end a relationship correctly. How many people reading this book still remember how emotional it was to say good-bye to dear childhood friends and how many may still have tokens of those good-byes?

What's next?

The source of adult success or failure in relating to others can be found in childhood. Children must learn skills to negotiate choosing, beginning, deepening, and ending relationships. Learning about relationships takes place first within the adult-child attachment relationship and then moves on to interactions with peers. Children's abilities to form relationships depend to a great extent on how old they are. It is important not to expect too much from children's attempts to relate to others. Don't push them too hard to relate to others in ways that are inappropriate for their stage of development.

In the next chapter we describe the communication skills children need to interact with others successfully. With these skills, children will begin to be able move more smoothly through the four relationship phases.

CHAPTER II

THE LANGUAGE OF RELATIONSHIPS

❋

How language works

Nonverbal communication and relationships

Major types of nonverbal behavior

Remember Jimmy, our Packer Backer from chapter 1? We left him happily playing with the boys on the playground. Jimmy had gotten the relationship ball rolling and was well on his way to making new friends. How exactly did he do that? How did he fit so smoothly into a new group of peers that his new play-mates felt good about having him join in? We've met adults who, like Jimmy, make us feel comfortable and at ease right from the start. We've also encountered others who, for some reason, are so annoying we just can't wait to get away from them. How do the pleasant folks who put us so at ease differ from those others who irritate us? Is it the way they look? What they talk about? How smart they are? Or are they just lucky?

Actually, luck has very little to do with success or failure when it comes to dealing with other people. We believe that Jimmy's success, and the interpersonal success of others, is due primarily to what is learned about communicating effectively. Using these skills, Jimmy will be as successful in deepening and ending his relationship with this new group of boys as he was in choosing and beginning it.

The term "communication" in this book means much more than the ability to read or speak words. We expand the meaning of communication to include the skill to send and receive non-verbal as well as verbal messages containing both intellectual and emotional information. By nonverbal language we mean every-thing that communicates meaning aside from the written or spoken word. This includes facial expressions, tone of voice (also called paralanguage), postures, gestures, use of personal space, touch, rhythm, and "objectics" (what we put on ourselves to communicate—hair styles, clothes, tattoos, etc.). Though non-verbal and verbal communication have many things in common, it is how they differ from one another that makes nonverbal communication so valuable when it comes to relating to others. If you are also adept at words, all the better, but without nonverbal skills, relating successfully to others would be all but impossible.

Though a bold statement to make, we believe that being able to send and receive nonverbal information accurately is probably the single most important basic skill we need to get along with others. People and animals both possess the ability to communicate nonverbally, but our uniquely human ways of using nonverbal communication make it essential for the relationship process.

As nonverbal expert Thomas A. Sebeok (quoting anthropologist Gregory Bateson) puts it so eloquently:

> ...not only did our nonverbal aptitudes and the organs that execute them *not* undergo conspicuous decay (during evolution), but, on the contrary, we preserved, perfected, and elaborated them "into complex forms of art, music, ballet...and the like, and, even in every day life the intricacies of human kinesic communication, facial expression and vocal intonation far exceed anything that any other animal is known to produce."

How language works

A language is a set of symbols whose meanings are agreed on by those who use them. We can use the word "ball" to communicate to others about a ball without actually having that object in our hands to show them. The word acts as a symbol or sign for that object. It is easy to understand how verbal language works. Less obvious is that nonverbal signs can function much like words do. For example, just as the word "smile" is a sign for the emotion of happiness, a physical smile is an external sign for an internal state of pleasure or joy. Nonverbal signs can be clearer and more powerful than words, especially when they reflect feelings. While every verbal language has different words for smile, the actual behavior of smiling is accepted as a sign of happiness across most all cultures and across past and present time.

All languages have receptive and expressive components. To receive, we must learn to decipher or decode the meaning of signs and symbols that others send to us. In verbal language this means trying to figure out the meanings of written or spoken words. Significant difficulty in accurately reading word cues and signs is called dyslexia (*dys* = inability; *lexia* = verbal signs or words). To express something, we must send or encode meaningful signs and symbols to others. In verbal language this is done by speaking and writing. Serious deficits in the ability to generate and use appropriate words—for instance, being able to identify fingers on a hand, but not being able to come up with the word "hand"—are often called expressive aphasias.

Just as verbal language has receptive and expressive aspects, so does nonverbal language. Receptive nonverbal language skill refers to the ability to accurately perceive the nonverbal cues of others by, for example, looking at their facial expressions or listening to their tones of voice. The important companion skill to receiving nonverbal information is learning to express the appropriate nonverbal cues through a variety of channels.

Some people have mild or serious difficulties receiving or sending verbal cues; likewise, some have trouble receiving or sending nonverbal language cues. We have coined the term

dyssemia (*dys* = inability; *semia* = to read or send signs) to refer to these deficits. There can be **receptive dyssemias** (difficulties in reading nonverbal cues) or **expressive dyssemias** (deficits in sending nonverbal cues) in any or all of the nonverbal channels.

Nonverbal communication and relationships

GLORIA

✳ ✳ ✳

Gloria is a cute six-year-old girl. She is wonderfully verbal and loves to chat with everyone she meets. On Tuesday she goes shopping with her mother. Gloria is excited; when she's excited she talks—to her mother or anyone else around. Mother and Gloria have a great time shopping. Around four o'clock, they decide to get a snack at the restaurant on the top floor of the department store, which is accessible only by elevator. As the mother and daughter enter the elevator, the four passengers already there rearrange themselves so everyone will have an equal amount of space. When the doors close, Gloria's mother and the other four adult passengers raise their heads and watch the changing floor numbers. Everyone is looking up except Gloria. Instead, she turns around and stares at the passengers. Before long she asks what they are looking at. Her mother tries to shush her but is unsuccessful. She apologizes to the other passengers, who are understanding. Gloria's mother, however, knows that her daughter's behavior is making them all uncomfortable.

What happened on the elevator?

Gloria may know some of the rules about appropriate verbal

behavior in closed spaces with others (don't yell, don't use rude words), but she hasn't yet learned that there are also special nonverbal rules to be followed in this situation. The inability to read nonverbal signals can cause problems, but fortunately most adults make allowances when children break rules. Because Gloria is relatively young, the negative reactions of the others are mild. Had she been ten years of age or older, the adults in the elevator would have expected her to know better and probably would have let her know of their disapproval, either nonverbally or perhaps even verbally.

The incident in the elevator reveals several important differences between nonverbal and verbal communication. First, whenever the verbal and nonverbal messages do not agree in emotional tone, we almost always believe the nonverbal one. Gloria's mother recognized that the passengers' nonverbal behavior did not match with their verbal responses. Her daughter's nonverbal behavior (looking at others while riding in an elevator, a serious breach of nonverbal language rules) was upsetting to them. Although the passengers reassured the mother that "everything was okay," their facial expressions, postures, and tones of voice told her that her Gloria's behavior was not acceptable.

Nonverbal cues are not only more likely to be believed, they are also more continuous than verbal ones. While the elevator passengers said very little, their nonverbal messages were continuously being sent and received. As relationship expert Paul Watzlawick mused, "you cannot not communicate nonverbally." Our own and others' faces, postures, and gestures never stop communicating information, and we never stop being affected by them.

Compared to verbal communication, nonverbal communication is also more likely to take place without our being aware of it. While we are aware of the words we and others use, we often are less conscious of the rich interplay of facial expressions, tones of voice, postures, and gestures that accompany those words. Gloria is no doubt aware of the words she uses every day. She knows that certain words are polite and that others are inappropriate in public. But in the elevator she isn't sufficiently aware of the nonverbal cues she is sending, and she's seemingly oblivious to the many nonverbal cues others are sending her.

The impact of rule breaking in verbal communication is different from that in nonverbal communication. When someone breaks a verbal rule of language, such as using a singular verb with a plural subject ("We was there."), the person risks evoking a negative intellectual response from others. We may think someone who makes that kind of mistake is not very smart or well educated, but we probably wouldn't have much of an emotional response to the person making the error. However, breaking a nonverbal rule of communication—Gloria stares at the people in the elevator rather than looking away from them—usually has a more negative emotional impact on others. We feel uncomfortable in the presence of someone who is breaking nonverbal rules of communication, but ironically, because most nonverbal communication takes place out of our awareness, we may not always be conscious of the source of our discomfort.

Insights into the problems that children may encounter in forming relationships are often discovered in the four differences between nonverbal and verbal communication:

- nonverbal cues are more likely to be believed
- nonverbal cues are more continuous
- nonverbal cues are more likely to take place without our full awareness
- nonverbal cues are more likely to produce an emotional response

Children with dyssemias can provoke negative emotional responses from others, provoke them continuously, and yet be unaware that they are causing these negative reactions. We call this set of difficulties inherent to nonverbal deficits the **dyssemic core,** and we suspect that it causes many personal and social problems.

A final difference between verbal communication and nonverbal communication is that they are learned in different ways. In contrast to the formal and direct training we receive through parents and teachers to read and write words, we learn nonverbal communication skills indirectly and informally, primarily by watching others. Because our educational system and society give us constant and direct feedback about our reading and writing skills, most of us generally know our verbal strengths and weaknesses. It is a much different picture for nonverbal abilities.

Through our research we have found that most people don't know how capable they are nonverbally. We know this because we have asked individuals how good they think they are at perceiving nonverbal cues or expressing themselves nonverbally. We then tested them and found that they, more often than not, tended to overestimate their nonverbal skill levels. That most of us are not as adept nonverbally as we think we are means that we already have one strike against us when we interact with others.

Six-year-old Gloria had an opportunity to learn about nonverbal communication by paying attention to what went on between her mother and the other passengers in the elevator. If she observed that her mother's admonition to shush occurred as the other passengers' facial expressions were communicating negative emotions, Gloria might have connected her behavior and their negative reactions. Of course, Gloria's mother could have made her daughter aware of the nonverbal messages directly, but (like most of us), she might not have been conscious of the interplay occurring or, even if she were aware of it, she might not have taken time at that moment to teach her child. Similar to most other children, Gloria will probably need to learn many of the associations between nonverbal cues and emotions herself.

In our other books and in our research we have made the case that significant nonverbal errors can produce personal and social problems for children and adults. People who make nonverbal errors often make them *continuously*; such errors have a *negative emotional impact on others*; and—even more crucial—*these individuals may not even be aware they are creating trouble for themselves*. Furthermore, it is probable that few of us *will directly and formally teach anyone how to avoid such errors*. Socially successful children must know how to communicate nonverbally as effectively as they use words. With awareness of—and skill in—nonverbal communication, children will find social relationships more attainable and much less mysterious, confusing, and stressful.

Major types of nonverbal behavior

To form and keep good relationships, children must master six major categories of nonverbal communication: facial expression, paralanguage, personal space, touch, posture, and gesture.

FACIAL EXPRESSION

Faces always catch our attention. Watch a six-month-old's eyes as someone passes by. Does she look at the person's legs, arms, hands, or shoulders? No! The infant will instantly focus on the face. When two people interact, they spend more time looking at one another's faces than anywhere else. Early in life, as soon as the child's neurological development allows, parents and infants are often found locked in eye-to-eye contact. The appearance of social smiles at around six weeks gives infants a powerful reinforcer to keep adults in contact with them. Smiling continues to be important as children grow older; it's so important, in fact, that a primary characteristic of popular children is that they smile more than their peers. Because sending and receiving accurate facial expression information is central to most relationships, even slight problems in processing that information can cause significant interpersonal difficulties.

Expressive and receptive facial communication. The face is the place for gathering and sending valuable social information. In almost every interaction, people exchange a steady stream of information about their attitudes and feelings through their faces. When you want someone to tell you the truth you don't ask them to "Look you in the foot"; rather, you say, "Look me in the eye." That is why it is so important to be good at reading and expressing emotions in faces. Learning facial cues that signal basic emotions—happiness, sadness, anger, fear, disgust, and surprise—forms the foundation for the later ability to recognize and express other, more complex social emotions such as guilt, embarrassment, and jealousy. If infants and children fail to learn how to read and express the basic emotions, it compromises their ability to learn more complex emotions later on. And because most basic emotions are learned within the parent-child relationship, it is essential for parents to be good teachers of nonverbal skills.

Early developmental errors, such as failing to learn to identify basic facial expressions, can increase the likelihood of relationship problems. If not corrected, such errors can contribute to the development of relationship problems in children and adults.

For example, a preschool student is at a disadvantage if he cannot accurately read the stern face used by teachers (and at times, by his parents) to command his attention and stop his present activity. Because he can't read this often-used expression, he could anger his teacher because she might mistakenly assume that he is being oppositional. Because of his receptive deficit, he is experiencing the dyssemic core: having a negative impact on someone, having it each time the face is given, and being unaware that he is causing a negative response.

To get along with others successfully, children not only must learn to read facial expressions accurately, but they also must learn to *send* facial expressions accurately. We know some children who do not vary their facial expression even when their feelings change. We've taken photos of them after we asked them to show different feelings through their faces, but all the photos look the same. Socially successful children can vary their facial expressions to show how they are feeling. When they are feeling happy, they look happy; when they are feeling sad, they look sad. It is easy to see where you stand with such children and, as a result, relating to them is easier and more fun.

The resting face. The resting face is the facial expression you wear when you are not feeling anything in particular. It is how your face looks when you and your feelings are neutral. Although our resting face isn't supposed to communicate particular emotion, in about a third of us, it does. Resting faces can communicate positive feelings or negative feelings of anger, sadness, or fear even when a person is feeling neutral. Negative feelings can be especially damaging at the choice and beginning phases of relationships. With whom would a person like to begin a relationship—someone who looks happy or someone who looks angry?

Smiling. Socially successful children in the United States are characterized by effective eye contact and smiling. These facial expressions were used effectively by Jimmy, our Packer Backer from chapter 1. He smiled at most everyone he met. Because his grin was irresistible, Jimmy got many smiles in return. The lesson is simple: if you want to make friends and get along with people, smile more.

Making eye contact and turn taking in conversation. Effective eye contact is just as necessary for social success as a smile. Studies of interactions show that we look at people more when we listen than when we speak to them. For example, in an ongoing conversation, we spend around 50 percent of the time looking at the other person's face. Inattention to facial expressions reduces the amount of information we pick up and can create confusion regarding turn taking in conversation.

Some children do not know when to speak in a conversation. They have a knack for saying the wrong thing at the wrong time and are often out of sync with their peers. Observing such children, we saw that they did not look at others, but rather averted their gaze when speaking or listening. Their peers never knew if these kids were receiving the cues they were sending. When children like this were coached and learned to improve their eye contact, others could tell when they were finished speaking and could tell when it was their turn to talk. With effective turn taking, friend-making capacity improved dramatically.

Intensity. Children need to be able to read and express facial emotional cues, smile a lot, and have effective eye contact; they also need to be able to modulate their expressive cues. Laughing too loudly when a joke is only mildly funny or not letting others know how much something is bothering you when you are upset can put off others and can contribute to social difficulties.

Horizontal zoning. Not all areas of the face are equally important when it comes to feelings. The eyes tell much more about emotions than any other part. So it makes sense that you should look into the eyes to pick up information. Autistic children, most of whom have serious relationship difficulties, for example, look at others' faces as much as non-autistic children do, but they mistakenly focus on the mouth rather than the eyes. This misplaced focus prevents them from gathering important cues about how others are feeling and puts them at risk for being rejected by others.

PARALANGUAGE

Paralanguage refers to all the aspects of sound that accompany words but are independent of words and communicate emotion. These features include but are not limited to tone, loudness, intensity of voice, and sounds uttered between or instead of words such as humming and whistling. Coupled with facial expression, paralanguage accounts for much of the emotional meaning carried between conversational participants. How we sound when we speak words is a crucial indicator of how we feel. To be successful interpersonally we must be able to identify the feelings behind the words of others and, in return, we must be able to express our emotions accurately with our voices.

The importance of paralanguage is often overlooked because of the more apparent cues being sent and received visually— facial expressions, postures, and gestures. But when the visual elements of human interaction are diminished or removed, such as when talking on the telephone or listening from another room, the importance of paralinguistic cues becomes more apparent.

Tone of voice. The importance of what we say is often outweighed by how we say it. Our tone of voice makes it possible for us to say with our words, "That's nice" while communicating with our sad tone that we don't feel nice at all. Tone of voice is basic. Infants can differentiate their mother's tone of voice from that of others three hours after birth; this suggests why tone takes precedence over spoken words when the two differ in emotional meaning.

Individuals who can vary their tone of voice have a huge advantage over others who speak in a monotone and convey a smaller spectrum of emotions. These people communicate more fully how they are feeling and what emotional reactions they desire from others. In contrast, listening to someone speak in a monotone and trying to figure out how he or she feels can be discouraging, irritating, and even maddening.

CHANDRA AND ASHLEY
✳ ✳ ✳

Chandra calls her third-grade classmate, Ashley, about a play date. "Hi, Ashley," she says in a bright voice.

Ashley answers in a low monotone, "Hello."

"Do you want to come over to my house after school tomorrow?"

"Sure," Ashley responds in the same low monotone, "that would be fun."

Now Chandra is puzzled, because Ashley certainly doesn't sound like she thinks it will be fun. In fact, it's difficult to know what, if anything, she's feeling. "Well," Chandra says, "why don't you think about it and call me back if you can come."

After she hangs up, Chandra shakes her head and says to her mother, "I don't think Ashley likes me. I don't think she wants to play at our house."

A note about sarcasm: When people are being sarcastic, they are intentionally communicating a discrepancy between their words and their tone of voice. For example, if you thought someone wasn't dressed particularly well you might say, "Nice outfit," with disdain in your voice. While the words convey a compliment, the contrary tone of voice suggests an insult. Sarcasm is a potentially hurtful form of paralinguistic communication. It is used mainly by adults and is very difficult for most children to grasp. Sarcasm should be used sparingly if at all with children.

Nonverbal sound patterns. Infants and toddlers use a variety of sounds and noises to communicate their feelings and desires to adults. These sound patterns are a major method of communication between parents and children. Although the frequency and use of these sounds decrease as children become older, many of these sounds retain their communicative value even into adulthood. People of all ages use inflection to vary the meaning of a sound. *Huh-uh* said with the second sound higher than the first means, "Don't you do that." *Ohhh* said with a higher inflection as the sound goes on means "Isn't that interesting," but the same *Ohhh* said with a lower inflection as the sound goes on means "I am so disappointed." It is important that adults pay attention to and become proficient at interpreting and expressing these sound patterns so they can connect with their young children and teach them other nuances of nonverbal language.

Rate of speech. Various tones of voice and sound patterns communicate emotions, and so does the speed of talking. We all have a preferred rate of speech. Some of us naturally speak slowly; some of us talk quickly. But to be socially effective we need to be flexible enough to speed up or slow down our talking pace in different situations. Our rate of speech may even evoke a feeling in others that we did not intend. Individuals who talk exceptionally slowly can give the impression of being hesitant and insecure and, if they speak in a monotone, can bore their listeners. In contrast, fast talkers can place intense demands on others and give the impression that they are—and want their listeners to be—in a hurry. Parents need to be especially aware of their rate of speech when interacting with their children. They need to modulate their rate of speech to match the rhythm of their children's needs when they can. When a child is tired and unhappy, for example, a parent may find that a slow, soothing rate of speech may be a much more helpful way of communicating. Through such synchrony, parents and children become more connected, and nonverbal language learning can be accomplished more effectively.

PERSONAL SPACE

Like most other animals, humans are territorial. Unlike animals who mark their territory biologically, humans tend to mark physical territory with fences or signs. Territorial concerns play a big role in our lives from the international level to that of the neighborhood. Even our most popular team sports such as football, basketball, and soccer are about territory—one team defends its turf against the other. But we humans also recognize—either consciously or unconsciously—a more personal type of territory. Understanding the meaning of personal territoriality—personal space—and how it works is essential to forming good relationships.

Personal space refers to our own portable territory or "bubble" that we carry around with us everywhere we go. The bubble surrounds each of us. It is wider in the back than in the front, and contracts or expands depending on the social context and situation. When someone approaches us too closely, we are alerted to a potential danger: Is this person close enough to harm us? There is no quicker way for others to offend us than to intrude too closely on our personal space—and no quicker way to offend others than by intruding on their space. Very strict rules exist about exactly how to approach the personal space of others and how to respond when other people venture into our own.

Research has shown that people recognize four major personal space zones.

1) The first and closest area is called the **intimate zone**; it begins at touch and extends out to about eighteen inches. Within this space, it is appropriate for intimate topics to be discussed and for close friends and relatives to approach.

2) Beyond this area is the **personal zone**, which extends from about eighteen inches to around four feet. In the United States, this is the distance at which most personal conversations and interactions with friends and acquaintances take place.

3) The **social zone** begins at four feet and ranges out to about twelve feet. Louder talking and less personal and more public interactions can take place in this space. It is inappropriate for intimate and personal matters to be discussed at this distance.

4) The final area is called the **public zone**, which begins at twelve feet and reaches to infinity. Public speeches are usually the only verbal conversation that is acceptable in this zone and, because increased distance makes perceiving facial expressions and tones of voice difficult, postures and gestures are the major nonverbal communication channels used in the public zone.

Failing to follow the restrictions of these zones can create difficulties. One common personal space error is standing too close to others. You've probably met close talkers—people who stand too close to you when they talk and don't seem to notice how uncomfortable, or even violated, their intrusion might make you feel. Another common error is discussing intimate topics in non-intimate zones. You might also have known people who inquire about intimate aspects of your health by shouting to you from across the room. Most of the time, such people don't seem aware that they are making you uncomfortable by talking about private issues in the public space.

Personal space mistakes can have more or less negative impact depending on the age of the offender. Toddlers break all kinds of space rules, but they cause minimal discomfort in others because children this young are nonthreatening. However, the same personal space error that causes minimal discomfort when committed by a two-year-old can become a serious blunder when committed by a ten-year-old who is expected to know (and to operate under) the same personal space rules as adults. That is why it is so important for children to learn about personal space by the time they complete elementary school.

A final note about personal space acknowledges the role of culture. The size and flexibility of the personal space bubble varies dramatically from culture to culture. Because of these variations, individuals from different cultures can easily violate one another's personal spaces. For example, European Americans generally have a much larger personal space bubble than Latin Americans. It might be difficult for members of these two cultures to find a comfortable conversational distance with one another. As the number of people from divergent cultures in the United States increases, awareness of the importance of personal space rules within and between cultures becomes more important.

Touch

Human beings need to be nurtured, held, and touched as infants and later as adults to know that they are loved and cared for. There are more stringent rules about how, where, and when to touch one another than there are about personal space. In part, this may be because being touched inappropriately is associated with sexual misconduct or physical abuse.

The subtlety and complexity of appropriate touching behaviors is illustrated by the unspoken rules that govern how we touch —or do not touch—someone if we are approaching from behind. One of the few acceptable ways of touching in this situation is to use the forefinger to lightly tap the person on an area of about a one square inch that is equidistant from the neck and the end of the shoulder. To touch heavily rather than lightly, or to touch somewhere other than the one-inch area would probably startle or frighten the person and get the interaction off to a bad start.

There are also strict rules for how and when to touch inside or outside the bodyline. Touching inside the bodyline—that is, inside the outline of the body—is relatively rare because it signals intimacy and has the potential to make people feel threatened. Socially successful children and adults must learn how to appropriately touch, pat, squeeze, brush, and stroke others and how to interpret other people's touching behavior. If young children have difficulty with either expressive or receptive touch skills (e.g., how to hug), they can be taught directly how best to touch others and how to accurately perceive the touch of others. These rules will differ from culture to culture.

POSTURE

Posture is known as the long-range nonverbal channel because it can communicate dominance, submission, and other attitudes or feelings at a distance. Posture refers to how we hold our torso, our hands and arms, and our feet and legs. Of all nonverbal behaviors, we are least aware of our postures. Postures often disclose how we feel even when we don't intend them to. Teachers claim they often can tell what kind of day they are going to have by the postures of their students. If the children are sitting up straight in their seats, the teacher can look forward to a productive learning day. If the kids are slouched down behind their desks, the prospects aren't so encouraging. Similarly, parents can get a head start on understanding where their children are emotionally if they pay attention to the way they present themselves and sit at breakfast.

Just as the resting face is important when establishing relationships, resting posture can also have a significant impact on interacting with others. Resting posture is the comfortable standing or sitting posture we assume when we are not feeling anything in particular. A resting posture can communicate negative emotions and attitudes even when we are not feeling them. If a child's resting posture is characterized by slouching and downcast head and eyes, she may be inappropriately communicating disinterest or irritation when in fact she is in good spirits. In contrast, a child who stands or sits upright with head and eyes forward may feel uninterested but appear to be happy, alert, and ready for new experiences. What the resting posture is communicating, especially at a distance, significantly affects whether we choose to approach or avoid someone at the choice and beginning phases of relating.

A final note about posture concerns posture in motion, or walking. Our way of walking can communicate much about us and our feelings. We applaud actors who excel at using a jaunty step or a sultry swagger to convey a mood or a feeling. Yet most of us are unaware of the fact that the way we stand and walk expresses how we feel whether we want it to or not. One walking skill is the ability to adjust our walking speed to suit the social context we are in or the people we are with. For example, a rapid, no-nonsense walk might be appropriate in a large city, while a slower more casual pace might be best in suburban or rural settings.

Parents and children are often at odds about pace of walking; kids may run ahead when they're on the way to a playground, but lag behind when they're shopping. As much as possible, parents should try to adjust the speed and rhythm of their walking to that of their children and use the instances of mismatch as opportunities for teaching nonverbal skills.

Gestures, Objectics, and Rhythm

Less obvious, but by no means less important in communicating with others, are gestures, objectics, and rhythm. Dyssemias in these nonverbal channels can create unique interpersonal difficulties for children.

From the simple act of waving "bye-bye" that we learn as infants to the more complex finger and hand movements that are part of all adult conversations, the gestures we make are important in directing and dictating moment-to-moment interactions. Adults have command of literally thousands of gestures, but most of the time they are not aware of them.

Gestures can function as batons to emphasize, complement, or specify the meanings of words. For example, the angle at which you hold your hand connotes how strongly you feel about signaling an approaching person to stop. To amplify your wish that the other person stop, you can move your hand—your baton—back and forth.

Some gestures embellish words; some are substitutes for words. In most cultures, moving the head up and down communicates "yes" while shaking it from side to side means "no." Crossed arms in front of the chest say "I am not convinced," while sticking out the tongue signals defiance.

Effective communication requires that words and gestures match. Asking someone to come closer while holding your fists clenched at your side can be confusing. Because nonverbal communication usually has more impact than verbal, the person probably won't come closer. Children need to know when and where to use gestures appropriately. High fives and pats on the back may be appropriate on a playing field, but probably are out of place in a more formal setting like a classroom. The more we make our children aware of how gestures affect their interactions, the better the chances are that their interactions will be positive.

Though most nonverbal behaviors are not deliberate, that is often not the case for objectics: the nonverbal communication channel having to do with how we look and what we put on (e.g., cosmetics, clothing, jewelry, hair styles, perfumes, and deodorants) to communicate our attitudes and feelings. Objectics are nonverbal signs whose meanings can rapidly change in contrast to the generally more permanent meanings of other communication channels. A smile is a smile for all time, but the significance of what you wear may change frequently.

When it comes to the area of clothing and jewelry, we are more interested in having children dress well with a good sense of self, than in having them pursue the latest fads and fashion. We do not favor conformity, but rather believe that children should use their awareness of who they are to dress creatively in a neat, clean manner. Personal hygiene is another important aspect of objectics. In the United States, most people believe that clean hair, sweet breath, and fresh-smelling skin are essential to successful social interaction. Because children often do not understand the concept of hygiene as an activity or recognize the need to practice good hygiene, it is up to parents to teach these skills to their children and to ensure that they practice them regularly.

Rhythm is the earliest, most basic type of nonverbal communication. Studies have shown that a newborn infant can discriminate among rhythms, favoring rhythms similar to her mother's heart rate. Rhythm is important in its own right, but it also plays a part in determining the meaning of gestures, walking, and speech.

There is both receptive rhythm (the ability to recognize the meanings of others' rhythms) and expressive rhythm (the ability to adjust one's own rhythms to harmonize with others and accurately express specific feelings or attitudes). Making children aware of their own rhythms and the rhythms of others will provide them with a skill they can use the rest of their lives. We all tend to enjoy being with someone who shares our rhythm and will avoid another whose rhythm does not fit ours. Parents need to become aware of their children's natural rhythms (and their own) so they do not inadvertently create stress and discomfort by working against them.

What's next?

Relationships go through stages of choice, beginning, deepening, and ending. Different communication skills, especially nonverbal ones, are needed to make transitions from one phase to the next successfully.

In the following chapters, we look at how the relationship process develops and changes over the course of time—from infancy, to childhood, to the juvenile period, and finally into preadolescence. What children learn at each stage of development forms the foundation for what must be learned at the next.

We move now to infancy, where the initial relationship process begins.

CHAPTER III

INFANCY
(BIRTH TO TWO YEARS)

✳

Order and predictability

A sense of self

A secure attachment relationship

What a child should learn during infancy for forming healthy relationships:

- To become aware of the order and predictability of things around him
- To form a sense of self
- To develop a secure attachment with an adult

Order and predictability

HANNAH RUTH

✳ ✳ ✳

Steve is looking at his granddaughter Hannah Ruth for the first time. It's about an hour after the baby was born. He and his wife Kaaren stand at the window peering in at seven or eight newly born infants. Some are nearly bald; others are curly haired. Some are quiet and some are screaming. The nurse asks their names, then moves to one of the cribs and picks up a red-faced, sparkly eyed, dark-haired baby and mouths the words, "This is yours."

"Look," says Kaaren. "Hannah Ruth is smiling at us."

Steve knows social smiling doesn't begin until at least six weeks, so he knows his wife is wrong. But for that moment he isn't a scientist, he's a grandfather. If a passerby should happen to stop and ask him what's going on, he'd readily

*claim that their new granddaughter is so glad to see them
that she's smiling at them from the other side of the window.*

Newly born infants are relatively helpless bundles of biological drives. They have little actual awareness—the world outside must seem like a seamless, timeless blur. During infancy, children change from completely self-absorbed individuals into social human beings who are aware of the social world and are active players in it. Only those relatively few children who suffer from disorders such as autism, schizophrenia, or severe depression stay trapped in their own inner worlds, unable to acknowledge or feel motivated to participate in social interactions.

The private inner world of the newborn becomes a more public one primarily through interactions with parents, who help infants learn about the social world by bringing order and predictability to the chaos they initially experience.

Developmental psychologist Richard Youniss describes this early time of life:

> Infants' actions of crying, sucking, and moving limbs result in contact with other persons and cause them to act in return. Other persons talk back, pick the infants up, or withdraw as they engage infants' actions. Were others wholly passive or simply benign, infants could center solely on their own actions. But others are also active and therefore infants can perceive order only through assessing their own actions in relation to actions of others.

Infants begin to learn about cause and effect—what is called **contingency**—through interacting with others. That is, they begin to be aware that what they do is associated with the way people respond to them.

LOCUS OF CONTROL

JASMINE

✳ ✳ ✳

As Jasmine finishes her bottle, her eyes begin to close. Thinking this is the perfect time to put her down for her nap, her father Jim tiptoes into the bedroom and carefully places his sleeping child into her crib. As soon as he steps out of the room, Jasmine lets out a howl of distress. Jim waits to see if his daughter might calm down on her own or cry herself to sleep after a few moments. When her crying continues, Jim goes back into her room. Within seconds Jasmine is in her father's arms and is quiet once more.

Jim, whether he knows it or not, is intimately involved in teaching his daughter about cause and effect (and she may be teaching him this same lesson as well). Learning about cause and effect helps to bring an infant out of her self-contained mental and physical cocoon and into the sunlight of the social world of others. Whether or not you perceive a connection between how you behave and what happens to you is a powerful learned expectation called locus of control (LOC), which is associated with academic, physical, and social success throughout life.

Locus of control is a psychological term that refers to how individuals perceive what happens to them. If they see a connection between their actions and what happens next, they are said to be "internally controlled." If, on the other hand, they fail to perceive connections between their behavior and what happens to them—and instead see what happens to them as a result of luck, fate, chance, or powerful others—they are said to be "externally controlled."

Many parents find that when they pick up and hold their crying infant, the infant stops crying. What's happening is that the infant is learning a contingency: "If I cry, someone will notice and take care of me." This is an important and powerful development in the baby's budding sense of control, along the lines of "I can make my needs known, and someone will respond." Many parents worry that by picking up a crying baby they may "spoil" the baby or give her too much control. This concern is sometimes exacerbated by well-meaning grandparents or friends who warn new parents of the dangers of giving in to the baby's wishes.

In our view, babies need to learn that they have some control. It's important for them to learn that they are seen and heard and considered capable of asking, often by crying or fussing, for what they need. What babies need, beyond feeding, changing, and sleep, is human contact—a soothing, physical adult presence. And often they cry until they get it! In fact, research shows that when parents respond promptly and sensitively to their baby's crying, the baby actually cries less by the end of the first year. So go ahead and pick up your baby.

Later on, as babies enter toddlerhood and gain some independence, they are ready to learn how to soothe themselves. At this point, parents' expectations regarding a child's capabilities will change. But for now, at least in the first year, picking up and soothing your baby is an important way to help her develop an internal locus of control. By the end of infancy (around eighteen months or so), children should have developed some sense that their actions play a part in what happens to them in their social world.

PARENT SKILL BUILDER

Observing a budding sense of control in your baby

Now that you know something about locus of control and how it develops, you can begin to observe signs that your baby is learning important connections between her actions and their consequences. You can watch this when your baby plays with toys. For example, notice what happens when you give your baby a rattle. The first shake will probably be accidental, as she doesn't yet know that she can cause the rattling sound. But watch the sense of surprise, then joy on her face as she discovers that she can make that sound happen all by herself! Many toymakers understand this fact and produce baby seats or mobiles that respond to a baby's movements.

To give you a better sense of what your own locus of control is and where you stand in terms of your own perspective, we've included an adult locus of control scale that you can fill out and score. Knowing more about your own LOC will help you be more aware of messages you are sending your children. Research shows that a person's locus of control can change, so if you wish your score were different, that's okay. You can change it! Think of the questionnaire as a way of sensitizing yourself to areas of your self-concept you may want to strengthen or develop.

LOCUS OF CONTROL SCALE FOR ADULTS

Different people will answer the questions on this scale in different ways. Don't take too much time answering any one question, but do try to answer them all, and try to pick yes or no for all the questions and not leave any blank.

One of your concerns during the test may be, "What should I do if I can answer both yes and no to a question?" It's not unusual for that to happen. If it does, think about whether your answer is just a little more one way than the other. For example, if you'd assign a weighting of 51 percent to "yes" and 49 percent to "no," then make your answer "yes."

YES NO

___ ___ 1. Do you believe that most problems will solve themselves if you don't fool with them?

___ ___ 2. Do you believe that you can stop yourself from catching a cold?

___ ___ 3. Are some people just born lucky?

___ ___ 4. Most of the time, do you feel that getting good grades means a great deal to you?

___ ___ 5. Are you often blamed for things that just aren't your fault?

___ ___ 6. Do you believe that if somebody studies hard enough, he or she can pass any subject?

___ ___ 7. Do you feel that most of the time it doesn't pay to try hard because things never turn out right anyway?

___ ___ 8. Do you feel that if things start out well in the morning that it's going to be a great day, no matter what you do?

___ ___ 9. Do you feel that most of the time parents listen to what their children have to say?

___ ___ 10. Do you believe that wishing can make good things happen?

___ ___ 11. When you get criticized, does it usually seem it's for no good reason at all?

___ ___ 12. Most of the time do you find it hard to change a friend's (mind) opinion?

___ ___ 13. Do you think that cheering, more than luck, helps a team to win?

___ ___ 14. Do you feel that it is nearly impossible to change your parents' minds about anything?

___ ___ 15. Do you believe that your parents should allow you to make most of your own decisions?

___ ___ 16. Do you feel that when you do something wrong there's very little you can do to make it right?

___ ___ 17. Do you believe that most people are just born good at sports?

___ ___ 18. Are most of the other people your age and sex stronger than you are?

___ ___ 19. Do you feel that one of the best ways to handle most problems is just not to think about them?

___ ___ 20. Do you feel that you have a lot of choice in deciding whom your friends are?

___ ___ 21. If you find a four-leaf clover, do you believe that it might bring good luck?

___ ___ 22. Do you often feel that whether or not you do your homework has much to do with what kinds of grades you get?

___ ___ 23. Do you feel that when a person your age is angry with you, there's little you can do to stop him or her?

___ ___ 24. Have you ever had a good luck charm?

___ ___ 25. Do you believe that whether or not people like you depends on how you act?

___ ___ 26. Will your parents usually help you if you ask them to?

___ ___ 27. Have you ever felt that when people were angry with you, it was usually for no reason at all?

___ ___ 28. Most of the time, do you feel that you can change what might happen tomorrow by what you do today?

___ ___ 29. Do you believe that when bad things are going to happen they just are going to happen no matter what you do to try to stop them?

___ ___ 30. Do you think that people can get their own way if they just keep trying?

___ ___ 31. Most of the time, do you find it useless to try to get your own way at home?

___ ___ 32. Do you feel that when good things happen, they happen because of hard work?

___ ___ 33. Do you feel that when somebody your age wants to be your enemy, there's little you can do to change matters?

___ ___ 34. Do you feel that it's easy to get friends to do what you want them to do?

___ ___ 35. Do you usually feel that you have little to say about what you get to eat at home?

___ ___ 36. Do you feel that when someone doesn't like you there's little you can do about it?

___ ___ 37. Do you usually feel that it is almost useless to try in school because most other students are just plain smarter than you are?

___ ___ 38. Are you the kind of person that believes that planning ahead makes things turn out better?

___ ___ 39. Most of the time, do you feel that you have little to say about what your family decides to do?

___ ___ 40. Do you think it's better to be smart than to be lucky?

Scoring Key on page 54.

Scoring Key

1. yes	9. no	17. yes	25. no	33. yes
2. no	10. yes	18. yes	26. no	34. no
3. yes	11. yes	19. yes	27. yes	35. yes
4. no	12. yes	20. no	28. no	36. yes
5. yes	13. no	21. yes	29. yes	37. yes
6. no	14. yes	22. no	30. no	38. no
7. yes	15. yes	23. yes	31. yes	39. yes
8. yes	16. yes	24. yes	32. no	40. no

Give yourself one point for every time your answer matches the one listed in the key.

What do your LOC scores mean?

Internal Scorers (0 to 8): Scores from zero to eight represent the range for about one third of the people taking the test. As a low scorer, you probably see life as a game of skill rather than chance. You most likely believe that you have a lot of control over what happens to you, both good and bad. You tend to take the initiative in everything from job-related activities to relationships. You are probably described by others as vigilant in getting things done, aware of what's going on around you, and willing to spend energy in working for specific goals. You would probably find it quite frustrating to sit back and let others take care of you, since your test answers stressed that you like to have your life in your own hands.

Although taking control of your life is seen by most people as the best way to be, psychologists caution that it has its own potential set of difficulties. Someone who is responsible for his or her own successes is also responsible for failures. So if you scored at this level, be prepared for the downs as well as the ups.

Average Scorers (9 to 16): Since you've answered some of the questions in each direction, your beliefs about internal and external control may be situation specific. You may look at one situation (work, for example) and believe that your rewards are externally determined, that no matter what you do you can't get ahead. In another situation (love, perhaps) you may see your fate as resting entirely in your own hands. You will find it helpful to review the questions and group them into those you answered in the internal direction and those you answered in the external direction. Are there any similarities in the kinds of situation within one of the groups? If so, some time spent thinking about what aspects of those situation make you feel as though the control is or is not in your hands can help you better understand yourself.

External Scorers (17 to 40): Scores in this range represent the external control end of the scale for adults. It has been found that only about 15 percent of the people taking the test score 17 or higher. As a high scorer, you're saying that you see life generally more as a game of chance or luck than one where your skills make a difference.

Introducing your baby to the concept of locus of control is an important first step in building skills that she will need to relate to others. Teaching your child to become aware that her behavior affects the way that others respond to her is a basic relationship lesson that you will build on as she matures.

Internal control in children is associated with a variety of positive outcomes. Studies show that internally controlled people—compared to their opposites, those who are externally controlled—are more likely to do the following:

- More actively search around for information that will help them solve their problems and reach their goals
- Remember helpful information and use it better
- Learn more intentionally and incidentally
- Engage in achievement activities more spontaneously
- Select more challenging tasks
- Delay gratification better
- Persist longer at tasks even when they are difficult
- Achieve better academically and vocationally

- Make more attempts to prevent and remediate their health problems
- Have better interpersonal relationships
- Be more respected and liked by others
- Be more resistive to being influenced by others
- Have better emotional adjustment as indicated by higher self-esteem, better senses of humor, less anxiety, less depression, and greater satisfaction and contentment with life

A sense of self

As they learn about contingencies, infants also begin to sense that they are separate from the faces and voices they see and hear around them. This rudimentary concept of self is gleaned from the reactions of others. "The reflected appraisals of significant others," said Harry Stack Sullivan, "not only helps infants to know they are separate from others but also whether they are good or bad people." If infants are comfortable and secure and see happy, smiling faces and hear friendly voices, they will learn to think well of themselves and begin to develop a positive self-concept. If, on the other hand, infants sense anxiety, hostility, and sadness in the reflected faces, voices, and touch of those caring for them, then they cannot help but be left with an impression that they may not be worthy individuals and will begin to develop a negative self-concept.

PETER

* * *

Peter is five months old. The babysitter doesn't show up,
so his father has to take the baby with him to a meeting

with his supervisor and the other advanced graduate students in psychotherapy. When Peter and his father walk into the office, the supervisor greets the baby and makes a funny face. Peter laughs and his round chubby face glows. When the supervisor holds out his hands, Peter smiles and goes to him readily, snuggling comfortably in the man's arms. "Peter must think he's something special," the professor says, smiling back at the baby.

"He is," Peter's father answers without arrogance or conceit.

Peter is well on his way to developing a positive self-concept. He is surrounded by smiling faces, warm soothing voices, and comforting experiences of touch that give him the impression that he is good person. Judging by the number and intensity of Peter's smiles, he agrees. Peter is also learning that smiling can bring warm, positive responses from the people around him.

Locus of control (see page 48) plays a part in the development of our self-concept. If we are to have a healthy sense of self-confidence, it is important for us to perceive that our actions have an appropriate impact on how the environment responds to us. However, having a sense of internal control can be a double-edged sword. A child being raised by a depressed mother, for example, may have difficulty developing a healthy self-concept. Because a depressed mother's reflected appraisals are generally negative regardless of what her children do, her children may grow up thinking badly of themselves because they may believe they have made her sad. Adults, especially those who serve as caregivers, must be aware of the emotional messages they give to children.

USING NONVERBAL LANGUAGE
TO BUILD A STRONG SENSE OF SELF

The emotional messages you send have a powerful effect on your baby's budding sense of self. Because many of the important emotional messages you send are nonverbal, it's helpful to know something about your own skill at conveying such messages.

Facial expressions. Almost from the moment infants open their eyes they are drawn to look at faces. As their ocular system matures, babies are better equipped to read facial expressions and use them as sources of social information. This means that long before they can speak or understand verbal language, babies use information they get from watching your face to gauge how you feel—and, more specifically, how you feel about them. Here are some exercises designed to help you increase awareness of the messages you convey with your face.

PARENT SKILL BUILDER
Awareness of facial expression

Babies need to see emotional information in our facial expressions. Research shows that babies become anxious when presented with a face that shows no emotion. This is because babies rely on our faces for feedback about potential dangers in their environment.

* Look at yourself in a mirror. Try to make facial expressions that accompany happy, sad, angry, and fearful feelings. Be sure to practice both low- and high-intensity examples of each feeling. Infants need large, exaggerated examples of emotions to help them learn. That is why you see good care-takers demonstrate extremely happy faces for their children to see. Some researchers have suggested that this kind of exaggerated nonverbal "talk" is inherited because it occurs

cross-culturally. Ask yourself what kind of emotional impact these different facial expressions might have on your baby.

✳ As an experiment, spend five minutes with your baby making different facial expressions and note how he reacts to them. If your baby is alert and engaged with you, you will notice that he will focus on what happens in your face, almost as if he's trying to make sense of what he sees.

✳ Make contact with your baby by smiling. Then, keeping eye contact, make your face completely expressionless and hold that look. In just a few moments your baby will turn away, try to engage you in emotional contact, or become upset. When this happens, regain contact by smiling and talking to him. This is a good way to remind yourself how important your facial expressions are, and it won't hurt your child in any way.

✳ Look at images of yourself that were taken when you were not conscious of the camera. (If possible, watch videotapes of yourself.) How do you come across? Is the image of yourself consistent with how you thought you looked and how you felt inside? Sometimes, it can be a surprise to watch ourselves! But it's terrific information about how we express ourselves nonverbally and how others see us.

Paralanguage. Babies become attuned to their mothers' voices very early in life. Although infants will not understand the words mothers speak, they will respond to the sounds. It is assumed that paralanguage—the tone, loudness, and intensity of voices—carries immense emotional information that infants can use to gauge signs of danger or delight. To see if your child has developed this skill and to help you become more aware of your own paralinguistic abilities, try these voice exercises.

PARENT SKILL BUILDER
Your voice and your baby

* Stand behind your baby on one side. Have a person with whom the baby is not familiar stand on the other side. Make sure you are both out of the baby's sight. Each person should call out the baby's name. If the baby has control of her head movement, she'll move her head in your direction.

* Sometimes it is difficult to know the impact of our own para-language. Record your own voice being soothing, angry, and sad. How do you sound? If it is difficult to tell the difference between your soothing voice and your sad or angry voice, practice making the difference greater.

Touch. Perhaps no type of nonverbal communication is more important during infancy than touch. Through touch infants learn to feel connected to the outside world. Infants are extraordinarily sensitive to the moods of their caretakers when they are being held. Held infants will know if you are anxious, tense, or angry. People in the United States are often character-ized as touch-deprived. We seldom touch others and are touched by others infrequently after the age of four. This means that many of us grow up not very adept at communicating through touch. Try these exercises to sensitize you to your own touch behavior and that of your child.

PARENT SKILL BUILDER
Touch and your baby

* Hold your baby as often as you can. Your infant will benefit from the physical contact. There are now several different kinds of baby carriers that make it possible to carry your baby and free up your hands. Some carriers are designed so the baby faces toward you; others are made so that the baby faces away from you. (Some can work either way.) Choose one that's appropriate for the baby's age (very young infants are too small and lack the head control to face outward) and that feels most comfortable to you. Some parents like to hold their baby in a sling. Options like these provide a terrific way to let your young infant have frequent physical contact with you.

* Spend at least five minutes a day gently passing your hands over your baby's skin. When you hold her, rub her back or massage her feet.

* Take a moment or two to consider your own feelings about touching others and being touched. It is important to be comfortable when you are touching or holding your infant; your discomfort will make her uncomfortable.

THE ADULT'S SELF-CONCEPT

Our self-concept—who we think we are—has great power to make us behave in certain ways with others. If we think realistically well of ourselves, we are going to enter relationships optimistically and look for the positive in others. In contrast, if we do not think well of ourselves, we will enter relationships with a predisposition to look for and pay attention to the negative. You can guess which of these two approaches will lead to successful relating.

While our self-concept develops throughout our life, much of it is learned during our early years, beginning in infancy. Most of the time we may not be aware of what we think of ourselves. Use the self-concept questionnaire below to take a look at the positive and negative elements you may have acquired over the years.

PARENT SKILL BUILDER
Self-concept measure

Knowing something about your own self-concept can help sensitize you to the development of your baby's. This questionnaire can help you assess how you think and feel about yourself. Chances are your self-concept will predict the self-concept of your baby. Remember to use the information not to judge yourself, but to learn about your strengths as well as areas you might like to change.

How do I think about myself?

Please answer the questions below honestly, using this scale:

SA = Strongly Agree
A = Agree
D = Disagree
SD = Strongly Disagree

___ 1. I feel that I am a person of worth, at least on an equal basis with others.
___ 2. I feel that I have a number of good qualities.
___ 3. All in all, I am inclined to feel that I am a failure.
___ 4. I am able to do things as well as most other people.
___ 5. I feel I do not have much to be proud of.
___ 6. I take a positive attitude toward myself.
___ 7. On the whole, I am satisfied with myself.
___ 8. I wish I could have more respect for myself.

___   9. I certainly feel useless at times.

___ 10. At times I think I am no good.

Score questions 1, 2, 4, 6, 7 by this scale: SA = 4, A = 3, D = 2, SD = 1

Score questions 3, 5, 8, 9, 10 by this scale: SA = 1, A = 2, D = 3, SD = 4

Add the total for all items on the scale. (Total scores will range from 10 to 40.) The higher your score, the higher your global self-esteem.

A secure attachment relationship

The most important goal for infants is to form a healthy attachment relationship with an adult, usually the mother. It is through this relationship that a child learns the most about who she is and her place in the world.

Failure to develop a good attachment relationship can have far-reaching negative effects. Without first becoming attached to an adult, children will find it difficult to develop the rich set of social relationships that will define them as adults. Infants who do not experience a nurturing and caring relationship with an adult are likely to develop psychological disorders, including—when the infant has little or no contact with a caregiver—a distressing state called "failure to thrive" in which the child stops eating, wastes away, and sometimes even dies.

Understanding that there is a connection between what you do and how others respond to you—and learning to see yourself as a separate "self" apart from others—sets the stage for the formation of the attachment relationship. Infants show rapid growth in cognitive and emotional abilities as they mature. Early on, they communicate with their mothers via nonverbal language: rhythm, facial expressions, tones of voice, and touch. A newborn falls to sleep more quickly to a metronome set at the rate of his mother's heartbeat than to any other rhythm. Three hours after birth, an infant can differentiate her mother's voice from the voices of others. By ten weeks of age, a baby can differentiate mother's happy, sad, angry, and fearful facial expressions. By two years of age, a child is capable of expressing and identifying an amazingly complex array of nonverbal emotional cues. The ability to understand and send nonverbal information provides the avenue through which an infant forms an early attachment relationship with an adult.

HOW ATTACHMENT RELATIONSHIPS DEVELOP

Much of our present-day knowledge about attachment relationships comes from the dedicated teamwork of John Bowlby and Mary Ainsworth. Bowlby was the first to describe what attachment relationships should be like, and Ainsworth developed ways to assess and then categorize how mothers and children relate to one another.

Bowlby believed that infants are born with a basic need to be with others and possess behaviors—like cooing and smiling—that pull for helping actions from adults. Successful attachment requires a generous mix of caring and nurturance from adults, regardless of the temperaments of the children.

Pre-attachment stage (birth to around two months). Although infants are assumed to be born with a basic need to interact with others, they aren't especially well equipped to do so initially. Parents, for all their smiles, song singing, chatting, and diaper changing, don't get much response from their infants at first. Things begin to change around six weeks, when infants usually begin to smile socially and turn their heads in the direction of the favored caretaker.

Attachment in the making (two to eight months). Once introduced to the process of social interaction, infants learn fast. Because they are especially nonverbally attuned to others, infants quickly home in on what's being communicated in faces and voices, especially those of their caretakers. It is not unusual to see infants and caretakers face-to-face, smiling and laughing. Infants need as much interpersonal contact and attention as parents can tolerate giving. Interaction with the primary caretaker is much preferred, although it is true that children also can comfortably interact with other adults.

Clear-cut attachment phase (eight months to two years). A clear-cut attachment relationship develops out of the complex and constant nonverbal negotiations that take place between the infant and caregiver concerning their mutual needs, preferences, and physical states. Adults use words when they communicate, but it is the vocal inflection, intensity, and volume that accompany the words—not their verbal content—that carry major communicative value for infants. Dependence on nonverbal communication may diminish somewhat at the end of infancy as children begin to acquire verbal language, but sending and receiving nonverbal emotional cues remains important throughout life.

During this stage an infant stakes out his claim to his mother and is upset when he is separated from her. Ainsworth is credited with the insight that the different ways children handle separation anxiety (when they are not with their mothers) reflect the relative health of the mother-and-child relationship. Perhaps even more importantly, the quality of this attachment relationship predicts to some extent how children will relate to others for the rest of their lives.

Infants and mothers both contribute to the attachment relationship. Attachment is categorized by how an infant reacts to being separated from, and then reunited with, the mother in the presence or absence of a young adult woman who is a stranger to them. Literally thousands of such observed and measured interactions revealed three general types of attachment that we'll call **secure, insecure avoidant,** and **insecure resistant**.

SHEILA

✳ ✳ ✳

Sixteen-month-old Sheila is brought by her mother to an orientation for children and parents at a daycare center. It is their first time there, and the mom holds her daughter as she walks around the room, looking at the colorful pictures on the wall. Sheila's eyes are wide. "Want to get down and have a look around?" her mom asks as she places Sheila on the floor near some blocks. Sheila resists being put down and lets out a howl of concern. It's clear that she is overwhelmed by everything around her and needs physical contact with her mother.

Mom responds by picking her up again, saying, "Okay, honey, let's walk around a little more while we both get used to this nice new school." After a few minutes, Mom notices Sheila is leaning away from her, looking intently at some toy animals in a bucket on the floor. "Want to try again, honey? Let's take a look at what's in here!" She places Sheila on the floor again, and this time Sheila is comfortable.

Before long, Sheila is completely absorbed in picking through the bucket to see what's in there. By this time, mom has moved to another part of the room and is talking with a teacher. Every so often Sheila looks over at her mom and holds up a little plastic animal she has found, as if to share her discovery. Mom responds with an enthusiastic "Wow!"

Eventually, Mom leaves the room to go to the teacher's office.

When Sheila notices her mom is gone, she begins to whimper and tries to follow her. An assistant approaches Sheila and directs her interest back to the animals, diverting Sheila's attention with a toy horse. When Mom returns a few minutes later, Sheila greets her excitedly and runs over to be picked up.

Secure infants use the adult caregiver as a safe base from which to reach out and learn more about their world. Only about half of all attachments in infancy are considered to be secure. When placed in a new situation, a securely attached child stays close to her mother and monitors her for information about the situation. If the mother signals safety, then secure toddlers, like Sheila, will soon set about exploring, pausing occasionally to check their mothers for signs of danger or approval. A secure infant shows few signs of anxiety or tension. If she runs into trouble, she returns to her mother briefly for comfort and then goes back to exploring. Although a secure infant is appropriately upset when the mother leaves the room, she usually finds ways to comfort herself until her mother returns. When she does, the child greets her mother enthusiastically, then returns to the business of finding out more about the interesting new place she is in.

HENRY

✳ ✳ ✳

Henry, fifteen months old, is brought to the same day-care orientation by his mom. But instead of walking Henry around the center and talking to him about all the new things to see, Henry's mom plops her son in the middle of

the floor and goes to find the teacher. She appears dis-
tracted. Henry seems unconcerned. He gets up, toddles over
to a small group of children playing with blocks, and grabs
a bright red block out of a little girl's hand. The girl howls
in protest. Henry amuses himself by banging the block hard
against the floor until an assistant comes and takes the
block away. When his mother re-enters the room with the
teacher, Henry hardly takes notice of her. He continues to
push a toy car around the room, seemingly oblivious to the
other children and adults who are present. When his mother
calls him to leave, he ignores her.

One type of insecure attachment relationship is called
avoidant. An avoidant infant and his mother appear to be largely
uninvolved and distant from one another. Although he may show
distress when the mother leaves, an avoidant infant pays little
attention to the mother when she returns. This contrasts dramatically with the behavior of a secure infant, who shows appropriate
distress when the mother leaves and happiness when she returns.
It appears that an avoidant infant fails to use the caregiver as a
source of security, warmth, and fun, but rather sees her as someone to be tolerated.

ISABELLA

✳ ✳ ✳

Nearly twenty months old, Isabella is also brought by her
mother to the daycare orientation. As they enter the room,
Isabella tenses up immediately. She tugs on her mother's
hand, as if to say, "I don't want to be here."

"Ow, let go of me," her mother responds. "You're hurt-
ing my arm!" Noticing Isabella's hesitance, the teacher
approaches with a coloring book and crayons. Isabella

shrinks back from the teacher. "Go on, Isabella, let's see you color," says Mom.

"Noooo," Isabella whines, "I don't wanna." She refuses to leave her mother's side. Her mother looks exasperated and worried. An assistant comes over to take Isabella while her mother leaves the room to speak with the teacher. Isabella begins to scream. Nothing the assistant does calms her down. The other children stop what they are doing and watch. Isabella is too upset to play or notice any of the interesting things in the room. When her mother returns with the teacher, Isabella approaches her, but is unable to stop crying.

A second type of insecure attachment is called **resistant**. The aloofness of avoidant infants contrasts markedly with the negative emotional behavior that characterizes resistant children. Instead of the barely tolerant acknowledgment of the mother shown by avoidant infants, those classified as resistant are more closely but more negatively tied to their caregivers. Resistant infants react with tears, anger, pouting, and whining when they are separated from their mothers and, surprisingly, also when they are reunited with them. Unlike secure infants, who also are upset by mothers' absence, resistant infants react more intensely when their mothers leave and take longer to calm down, if they calm down at all, when she returns. Although they act as though they desperately need their mothers when the mothers leave, resistant infants do not calm down when their mothers return. In this attachment relationship, mothers are valued but are not emotionally satisfying to the child.

The secure, avoidant, and resistant styles of relating that take root in infancy may grow into similar secure or non-secure attachment relationships in adults. Here's what Sheila, Henry, and Isabella might be like as adults if their childhood attachment styles persist.

SHEILA, TWENTY-FIVE YEARS LATER
✳ ✳ ✳

Sheila is now newly married. She has a strong, trusting relationship with her new husband, Dave. Although it is not a perfect marriage, Sheila has a fundamental trust in herself as a worthwhile person and is secure in Dave's love for her. She is confident in her ability to handle the ups and downs all relationships go through at times. Recently, for example, Dave has been undergoing a lot of job stress. He's required to work long hours, and he and Sheila have not had as much time together as they would like. When Dave has to cancel dinner plans at a restaurant, Sheila understandably feels let down. But she allows herself to feel her disappointment without criticizing herself for having these feelings and without blaming Dave for a situation that is beyond his control. After talking with a trusted friend about her feelings, Sheila sits down with Dave. She tells him that she misses spending time with him, that she understands his busy schedule, and that she feels she needs to reconnect with him again. Together, they plan to get away for a weekend in the coming month. At the end of their conversation, Sheila feels relieved at being able to talk about her feelings, and Dave has a good understanding of how she has been feeling. They both feel good about their talk and better connected to each other.

Secure infants freely explore the world of objects and people around them, learning much about how relationships operate. The trusting and reliable attachment relationships they have with their mothers provide a good model to use for future interactions with others.

HENRY, TWENTY-FIVE YEARS LATER
✳ ✳ ✳

Henry has grown into a handsome man who frequently attracts the attention of women. However, his relationships never seem to evolve beyond the beginning phase, and he is unable to deepen his attachments. His relationship with Molly falls into a typical pattern. He and Molly meet at a party and the attraction is instant. They date for a few weeks, and things are exciting. But when Molly begins to consider Henry a confidant and sees him as more than just someone to go out and have fun with, things change. Henry begins, in her words, "behaving strangely." He acts bored and distracted when they are together. He stops returning her phone calls. He is seen by a friend of Molly's at a restaurant with another woman. When Molly confronts Henry, he simply shrugs and says, "That's the way it goes." Molly is shocked that Henry appears to be so cool and removed. It's like he's a different person. Eventually, Molly stops contacting Henry. Henry's pattern is repeated with other women. When his friends question Henry about this pattern, he claims that he "just hasn't found the right woman yet." Meanwhile, he has developed a drinking problem.

In contrast to the rosy future for securely attached children, things don't look so good for their avoidantly attached peers who are more tenuously tied to others. Because they do not use their caregivers for feedback or comfort, avoidant toddlers have less opportunity to learn from them about social environments. Adults with an insecure avoidant relationship have fewer relationships, and the ones they have are characterized by distance and lack of emotion.

Isabella, Twenty-Five Years Later

✳ ✳ ✳

Isabella desperately wants to be married and have children. Like Henry, she has no problem meeting people to date. However, her relationships never seem to work out. Isabella drives men away with her constant need for attention and reassurance. Recently, for example, Isabella erupted in anger when Ron, her new boyfriend, forgot their three-month anniversary. Isabella was hoping that Ron would greet her with flowers when he picked her up for a date and was devastated and furious when he showed up empty handed.

"But Isabella, I'm here, aren't I? I may not have remembered that we met three months ago today, but I'm here and I'll take you out to dinner. What more do you want from me?" asks a bewildered Ron.

"If you loved me, you'd have remembered," Isabella retorts, tears streaming down her face. "Leave me alone," she cries as she gets out of his car and runs back into her apartment. Exasperated and put off by her behavior, Ron decides not to pursue her.

Late that night, his phone rings, waking him out of a deep sleep. It's Isabella, and she's crying again. "How could you drive off and just leave me there," she cries. "Why didn't you call me? Where have you been? How can you hurt me like this?" Ron knows that he cannot continue to be in a relationship with her.

Like adults who began as avoidant children, adults who were insecurely resistant attached infants will also find it difficult to form satisfactory relationships. However, it is their emotional volatility and anger that interferes with interactions, not a lack of desire to commit to a relationship. Resistant infants, unlike avoidant ones, seek attention from their caregivers, but once they have it they don't seem to know what to do with it. Resistant infants cannot strike the right balance between safely exploring their environment and feeling comfortable with the support and guidance of their mothers. Resistant children stand a good chance of becoming high-maintenance adults who attract others but have a difficult time keeping them close.

Goal-corrected attachment (around two to four or five years). The ultimate criterion for successful completion of the infancy phase of development is the presence of a secure attachment relationship with a caretaker. Nonsecure attachment is better than no attachment, but avoidant or resistant orientations will make it more difficult to successfully complete the relationship tasks of the next phase, Childhood. In calling the final attachment phase "goal corrected," Ainsworth reminded us that the flaws and failings of previous stages can be corrected. We agree. It is never too late to learn what was missed earlier in development.

There are many things you can do to promote a secure and healthy attachment relationship between you and your child. Try the following activities to foster a secure attachment in your baby. You can do them at any time during the attachment process.

Fostering a Secure Attachment Relationship
- **Tune in to your baby's emotional states.** Psychiatrist Daniel Siegel calls this resonance and defines it as occurring "…when we align our states, our primary emotions, through the sharing of nonverbal signals." The goal here is to perceive your baby's state (often by reading her face and

body) and respond appropriately—whether it's feeling and sharing in her excitement, understanding her frustration and being able to soothe her, or sensing her fear of a new person or situation and reassuring her.

• **Show sensitive responsiveness.** Research shows that babies who develop a secure attachment are those who have received what Ainsworth called sensitive responsiveness. This means being sensitive to your baby's signals and responding to his needs consistently. Don't worry that you are spoiling your baby. Research by Ainsworth and many others has shown that babies who can count on the fact that someone will respond to them in a caring and sensitive way are more likely to develop a secure attachment. They are also more likely to develop their own internal coping resources than babies whose needs are ignored or responded to in unpredictable ways.

• **See the world from your baby's perspective.** Remember that the world looks very different from the point of view of a little person who does not walk or talk. A few times a day, see if you can mentally shift gears and put yourself in your baby's shoes. Get down on the floor and look up at the playroom from the baby's perspective. Imagine yourself hungry, but with no way to tell anyone other than to cry. Imagine not being able to walk on your own and falling down for the tenth time. You'd like to get around as fast as the others in your family, but you can't seem to get the trick. Wouldn't you want to throw a tantrum? A one-year-old who cries hysterically after a fall is not trying to drive you crazy. He is, in the words of life coach and writer Martha Beck, a "very ambitious person in a very small body."

• **Don't hesitate to reach out for support.** Parenting babies and small children can be demanding and exhausting! You will be in a better position to give your baby the experiences needed for a secure attachment if you are in good emotional shape yourself. When possible, get someone to stay with the baby while you do something just for yourself. Talk to your spouse or a friend about your feelings about being a parent, the kinds of experiences you are having as a new parent, or even just what your day with your baby was like. Our brains are wired to share our inner experiences with others. It's especially important for new parents to do this as they navigate parenthood. If you can be heard, you are more likely to be able to tune into and sensitively respond to your baby's needs to be heard.

• **Know your own attachment style.** Your feelings about your baby's attachment needs are influenced by your relationship history and attachment style. Think about the different attachment styles we have described and consider which one is closest to the way you interact with others.

• **Observe your baby's attachment-related behaviors.** Now that you know something about the attachment relationship, you are in a better position to observe your baby's attachment behavior. Remember that an infant's attachment-seeking behavior varies with age and stage of attachment. Observations from early phases give clues regarding infants who stray from normal progress. The observations you make about how your baby behaves while in your presence, when alone, and with others can provide valuable information about the attachment process.

• **Take time every day to play with your baby.** Much of children's time is spent in play. Playtime can be an occasion for learning as well as for having fun. A great way for parents to nurture the attachment relationship is to take time every day to play with their baby (that is, once the baby is past the point where most of his day is spent eating, eliminating, sleeping, or crying). In addition to being enjoyable for its own sake, play is an important way to learn about relationships. Of course, little babies are too young to have play dates with peers (but when they do, it's so moms and dads can socialize with each other—an important thing for all parents). But there is much for babies to learn in the little day-to-day playful interactions they have with their parents and siblings.

What can babies learn from play?

SEAN
✳ ✳ ✳

Six-month-old Sean is sitting on a blanket on the floor, watching his mother Michelle fold laundry. His eyes follow her as she walks back and forth between the laundry basket and the dresser drawer.

"How ya doing, buddy?" Michelle smiles as she looks over at Sean.

"Coodlooo!" chortles Sean, his eyes big as he attempts to reach for the T-shirt Michelle is folding.

"Oh, you wanna get that? You wanna get that, honey?" asks Michelle playfully. She picks up the T-shirt and sits down with it in front of Sean. "Here you go, honey." Sean grabs it tightly in his fist and puts a piece of it in his

*mouth. Michelle watches for a moment, then says playfully,
"I'm gonna take it back!" as she smiles and gently tugs on
the T-shirt. "I'm gonna take it back," she says again, her
voice lilting with gentle enthusiasm. Sean laughs excitedly as
he pulls the shirt back and stuffs more of it into his mouth.
Giggling, Michelle tugs back.*

*This dance goes back and forth for a minute or two until
Sean pulls the shirt out of his mouth and looks away, as if
to say, "Okay, Mom, I need to rest now."*

A great deal has happened in this short, simple play interaction. First, most of the communication between Michelle and
Sean was nonverbal. Most relationships are built on nonverbal
communication, and this is especially true of the attachment relationship between parent and child. Here, Michelle picks up on
Sean's interest in playing with the T-shirt. She notices the look of
focus and curiosity on Sean's face as he reaches for the T-shirt.
She senses from his face and his forward-leaning posture that he
is alert and curious, and she takes the opportunity to engage him.

As they play with the T-shirt, Michelle tailors the back-and-forth game to Sean's level. Her play is gentle and she matches her
rhythm to Sean's, taking her cues from him. She notices the mischievous glint in his eye as he grabs the T-shirt from her, then
watches her expectantly as he waits for her to yank it back. She
correctly reads his joyful chortling and laughing as indications
that he wants more. Importantly, she also notices the shift in
Sean's mood as he stops the tug of war, becomes quiet, and looks
away. This is a likely signal that he has had enough play and needs
a break.

Sean is learning that when he sends a signal with his face or
body, or through a shout of enthusiasm, his mom can recognize

what he is saying and respond to him on his level. He's learning, through a brief, playful interaction, that someone understands him—when he laughs it means he wants to play and when he looks away it means he's had enough.

Finally, Sean sees that there's great fun in being with his mother. Sometimes, in their eagerness to optimize children's intellectual development by providing educational toys and gadgets, parents overlook the fact that what babies need most is simple: face-to-face, fun time with parents. It's these kinds of deceptively easy interactions that build up a healthy attachment relationship.

The best kind of play is interpersonal. No props or advanced training needed! The most important thing is that you rely on your baby's nonverbal communication to let you know when she's ready to play, whether or not the play matches her mood and capability, and when she's had enough.

PARENT SKILL BUILDER
Playing with your baby

* Put on some music and dance with your baby. Babies often respond to the rhythm in upbeat music—for many, being moved to the beat is a soothing rhythmic experience. This is also a fun release for parents!

* Babies benefit from and enjoy being talked to, especially in playful ways. Try having some fun with your own creativity and make up some nonsense rhymes for your baby. Don't worry about them making sense, just have fun! Nicholas, a young infant, laughs uproariously when his parents sing him this ditty they made up based on his name: "Nickadoo, Nickadee, Nickadye, Nickadoe. Nickadum-dum-dum, Nickadiddle-diddle-doe."

* A song that includes hand movements, like the "Itsy, Bitsy Spider," is often a source of great fascination for young babies and is a great way to interact with your infant.

* Sing to your baby. No matter how bad you think your voice is, your baby will love it!

* Take your baby outside and talk about all the interesting things you see. Don't worry if she can't yet understand what you are saying—she'll be thrilled to be outside, safe in your arms, feeling your joy and satisfaction while watching the trees and birds.

What's next?

The attachment relationship the infant forms with his primary caretaker—usually his mother—is his first true relationship, and it builds a foundation for those relationships yet to come. It requires time and effort on the caretaker's part to help the infant learn how to connect with another person and how to grow from being in a relationship with that person. Guiding a child to a successful attachment relationship is not only rewarding—it is also a lot of fun.

What is to be accomplished by the end of the infancy stage?

* To see the world as orderly and predictable
* To develop a secure sense of self
* To be securely attached to an adult

CHAPTER IV

CHILDHOOD
(TWO TO FIVE YEARS)

✳

Parents, children,
and the attachment relationship

Learning to relate through communication

Learning to relate through play

What a child needs to learn during years two to five for forming healthy relationships:

- To be aware that he is valued by mom and dad
- To be aware of his own and others' feelings
- To relate successfully with peers

Parents, children, and the attachment relationship

In Margaret Wise Brown's well-known children's story *The Runaway Bunny*, a little bunny decides to run away from home. As we read the story and see the pictures of this tiny bunny with grand plans for going it on his own, we wonder how he will survive away from his mother. But we quickly discover that for every plan the bunny has concocted, his mother has her own plan for keeping him safe. While she lets him talk about all the ideas he has for hiding on his own, she nevertheless comes back with a plan to be there for him, no matter where he hides. When he decides to become a bird and fly away from her, his mother tells him she will become a tree for him to come home to. When he wants to hide in a garden, she tells him she will become a gardener and find him. The message is clear. No matter what, this mother bunny is there for her son. The relationship is a safe place for him to come home to. This is the essence of the attachment relationship.

We liken children's early years to building a house. A well-built house needs a strong foundation. In relationship terms, that foundation is a secure attachment relationship with parents during infancy. Children continue to build on this base as they learn to develop new relationships with others, especially peers.

By the time children are two years old they are mobile, fairly well coordinated, and can do a lot on their own. They are beginning to use verbal language to communicate and are continuing to learn more about how to express and read nonverbal cues like facial expressions and tones of voice. The helpless infant has become a little boy or girl with a clearly emerging personality and a well-established place in the family.

Youngsters between two and five years of age are in the stage Sullivan called **childhood** (parents refer to this time as the pre-school years). As Sullivan saw it, during this period children are beginning to make connections with others outside of the family under the guidance of the parents. The most significant relationship in a child's life continues to be with the parent to whom the child attached during infancy. Through this relationship, a child continues to derive a sense of physical safety and emotional security, relying on the attachment relationship to learn more about the social world. It's important to note that parents set the tone here, not only for the attachment relationship, but also for other relationships their child begins to form with other young children. Parents are still clearly in control of their children's relationship interactions.

SETTING THE TONE FOR LEARNING HOW TO RELATE

Young children's early interactions with others outside the family occur under the watchful eye of the parents, who select preschools, arrange play dates, choose whose birthday parties to attend, and decide which playgrounds to visit. Even when children of this age are playing with peers, their parents are usually close by, ready to intervene or assist if necessary. Parents, the main supervisors of their children's daily activities, select and structure nearly all of their children's early relationships.

Later on, when children are in elementary school and have entered what Sullivan called the juvenile phase, parental control diminishes. Children become more independent, and parents have less influence over who gets selected as a friend and what happens in that relationship. However, that has to wait until the childhood phase is completed. The years from two to five are a key time for parents to pass on to their young child important basic skills concerning relating to others.

The attachment relationship can teach young children much about themselves and others, and fortunately they are usually eager to learn. Preschool-age children have an insatiable desire to understand the world. Is there any parent who has not heard questions like these? *Why? Why is the world round? Why do zebras have stripes? How do the wheels make the cars go? Where does the night hide when it's day?*

As we were writing this book, one of our sons, five at the time, asked, "How do they get the electricity into the computer wire so you can write on the computer? Were there computers when the dinosaurs were on the earth?"

As they begin to understand that the world is a big and often confusing place, children need to feel reassured that they are safe and protected. Who will help them find their way? The answer is their parents, using the attachment relationship.

Children's developing cognitive abilities and emotional knowledge lead them to want to feel valued—to feel noticed and appreciated. Trust us, children will notice whether or not your eyes light up when they come into the room.

HELPING KIDS MOVE
FROM DEPENDENCE TOWARD INDEPENDENCE

While we believe all parents want their children to feel accepted and valued, we also know that children can be demanding and exhausting. How exhausting? Well, researchers discovered that preschoolers demand something of their parents an average of three times per minute. (You can check this out for yourself—if you have time.)

One reason preschool children are a handful is that although they have made many strides toward independence and are often proud of their accomplishments, they are still physically and emotionally dependent. They need their parents. Children of this age struggle internally between the wish to be grown-up and the wish to be taken care of. One minute they want to put on a fancy dress to go shopping with the grown-ups and the next they may want to be talked to as though they were a baby. This struggle is a recurrent theme throughout childhood; for some children, it is an ongoing theme throughout the rest of pre-adulthood development.

Most of us have forgotten what it is like to be a three- or four-year-old. To a young child, although the world is a fascinating and exciting place, so many things are still out of physical reach and cognitive understanding. Every time a certain three-year-old was told she could not do what she wanted to do, she responded, "When I get bigger and bigger, I can." It is not unusual for a child who wants to be grown-up at one moment to dissolve into tears the next. This up-and-down behavior can be disconcerting to parents. We want you to know that not only is it normal for children of this age to act this way, but it is a healthy emotional reaction to learning about their strengths and limitations while still in the safety of an attachment relationship.

PARENT SKILL BUILDER

Getting in touch with how it feels to be a child

Take a breath, let your mind go, and see if you can come up with a memory from your own preschool years. Maybe it's a memory from home, a holiday memory, or a memory from daycare. Don't worry about how accurate your recollection is. The most important thing is to try and recall the feeling associated with the memory. Were you joyful, scared, mad, sad, or confused? Try to recreate such reactions and feelings in your mind.

Another way to tap into childhood feelings is to look at old photos or videos of yourself, maybe with one of your parents or a sibling. Choose an emotional occasion such as your first day of school or a birthday party. Again, see what feelings come to you. Hang on to them. They will help you understand your child's feelings.

CREATING A HOLDING ENVIRONMENT

What children need most from parents at this stage is what the late psychologist D. W. Winnicott called a "holding environment." This means parents need to be able to tolerate and accept the child's internal state, no matter what that is. It means helping the child learn to get comfortable with the full range of human feelings by being able to say, "It's okay to feel sad...or angry...or hurt," and to separate the feelings themselves from acting on those feelings.

While parents must sometimes disapprove of certain behaviors, they can still accept the child's feelings. Parents can convey this simultaneous disapproval and acceptance in what they say to their children. "I understand why you might feel angry at your sister for knocking down your blocks, but it's not okay to hit her." Or, "I will not let you throw your blocks against the wall when you are angry. Let's have you use your angry words instead. Tell me about how angry you feel." Messages like this build a strong sense of self-regard in a child. They help the child learn self-control at the same time that they convey the message that feelings can be felt, accepted, and handled.

Often just the very act of being able to name and talk about a negative feeling with someone who understands loosens the grip of a feeling on a child. (This is true for adults, too.) People get into trouble not when they feel and express their feelings but rather when they try to hide feelings or tell themselves not to think or talk about them. Research in the field of emotional intelligence tells us that children who turn out to be well-adjusted adults psychologically are those who are comfortable feeling and expressing a wide range of emotions. This is something that can be taught during the childhood stage of development if parents model what they want their children to do and encourage them to do it.

PARENT SKILL BUILDER
How to model effective expressing and handling of feelings

When you have a feeling, particularly a negative one, instead of squelching it or pretending you don't have it, stop. Take a deep breath. Remind yourself that you are entitled to your feelings! Find a name for the feeling that your child will understand. For example, "Daddy's feeling a little bit stressed right now." Then tell the child what you are going to do to handle the feeling. For example, "Daddy needs to sit down in a quiet place and breathe slowly for a while. That way, I'll calm down and feel better. Then I can spend some time with you."

FOSTERING A SECURE ATTACHMENT RELATIONSHIP IN YOUNG CHILDREN

Psychologist David Elkind calls the family the "first school of human relations." It is where important social lessons are transmitted from parent to child—lessons that children need to learn if they are going to successfully enter the society of full-time school and peers. The family, in the context of the attachment relationship, is where children form expectations of themselves and others that they will carry with them into the outside world and apply to their interactions with others. Children in a secure attachment relationship usually grow up to be adults who are able to maintain a strong sense of self, yet are able to extend themselves to others. Parents play a significant role in making this process a success.

It is so important for parents to understand children's internal, emotional experiences, to be able to see things through children's eyes and to be aware of what they are going through. We often forget that children experience the world differently than we do. Understanding a child's view of things has many benefits. Compare the responses of two parents whose children don't want to go to school.

KRISTEN AND JOE

❊ ❊ ❊

Kristen is getting her four-year-old son Joe ready for preschool. Joe is resisting.

"I don't wanna go to school today."

"You have to," says Kristen. "Now put your shirt on."

"But I don't wanna go," Joe whines. "I don't like to go there."

"Joe, you don't have a choice. Now hurry up."

"No," Joe whimpers. *"I don't wanna. I won't put my shirt on."*

"Put this shirt on right now! If you don't have it on by the time I count to three, I'll put it on you myself."

Joe dissolves in tears and lies down on the floor, refusing to budge.

Kristen is in a hurry. Assuming that Joe's resistance to getting dressed is merely a stalling tactic, she tries to push him past his reluctance. When he complains that he doesn't like to go to preschool, she makes no effort to find out why he is unhappy and rushes him even more. The interaction results in more delay when Joe has a complete meltdown.

MIKE AND CAITLIN

❋ ❋ ❋

"Daddy," says four-year-old Caitlin. *"I don't like school, I don't wanna go."*

"You don't?"

"No, Daddy. I don't wanna go back there. I wanna stay home with you."

Mike sits down on the edge of the bed with Caitlin. "Sometimes it's hard to go to school, isn't it?"

"Yeah," Caitlin agrees. *"I don't want to. I want to stay here and play with my toys."*

"Sometimes you just want to be at home with your own toys, don't you?"

"Yeah, sometimes I just like staying home." Caitlin looks up at her dad. *"Can I?"*

"I know it feels hard to go sometimes, honey." Mike pauses. *"But even though it feels hard, we still have to go.*

Here's what I want to do. I want you to help me think of something that would make it easier for you to go. What would help you go to school?"

"I don't know...I only wanna go if I can play with Jessica," Caitlin says. "Can you tell the teacher that I want to play with her?"

"How about if we both tell her?"

"Okay."

Notice that in his exchange with Caitlin, Mike tells his daughter that she has to go to school. He is clear about the rule. But unlike Kristen, he tries to see the situation from his child's perspective. He talks to her in a way that lets her have her experience of the situation, rather than talking her out of it. Once Caitlin feels understood, she is more willing to go.

PARENT SKILL BUILDER
Putting yourself in your child's place

Think back to a time when you were upset and someone understood your feelings. Maybe you were talking to a favorite aunt or uncle who picked up from your nonverbal behaviors that you were feeling overwhelmed with caring for your child and said something simple like "Sometimes it's so exhausting being a parent, isn't it?" and gave you a hug. How did you feel? Wasn't it wonderful that someone actually understood how you were feeling, accepted it, and didn't try to lecture you on how to better manage your stress? The feeling of relief that comes from being understood is something you want to convey to your children every chance you get.

Do realize, however, that it is quite possible Caitlin could have continued to protest, despite Mike's empathic statements.

Validating a child's experience is no guarantee that a child will suddenly see the light and immediately behave exactly the way the parent wishes. Parents must always keep the long-term goals in mind. More important than the immediate outcome is the long-term benefit for the attachment relationship and for the child's sense that her experience matters. Caitlin knows her dad is in charge and that he may make decisions she doesn't like, but she also knows he accepts and understands her feelings. Mike's response to his daughter embodies what parent-educator Rudolph Dreikurs called "kind and firm." Children whose parents practice being both kind and firm know what is expected of them and feel understood and valued. These types of interactions with their parents help children learn how to empathize with others.

PARENT SKILL BUILDER
Being the boss

By being able to accept and redirect, you can convey understanding and still be the boss while interacting with your children. First, work at simply accepting the behavior or feeling that the child is showing. For example, to a child who is jumping on the furniture you might say, "Sarah, I see how much you like jumping on the sofa." Then provide the child with a behavioral alternative. "But you'll have to do your jumping down on the floor."

To a child who has an angry outburst, say something accepting. "George, I can see how angry you must feel." Then say something redirecting. "Use your angry words and tell me about it." To a child whose feelings have been hurt by another but who is having trouble naming those feelings and deciding what to do about them, you could say something accepting and redirecting. "Eva, it must have really hurt your feelings when Michael called you a name. Let's use words to tell him that."

REPAIRING THE ATTACHMENT RELATIONSHIP

Despite parents' best intentions, things just don't always go the way they'd like them to. Children get cranky or act stubborn. Sometimes parents are exhausted, overwhelmed, or just plain too short on patience to deal with their children constructively. Sometimes parents wind up saying things or acting in ways they regret later.

DIEGO AND MARIA

✳ ✳ ✳

Five-year-old Diego is downstairs yelling for his mother Maria to bring him something to eat. She is upstairs in her office trying to get some work done on the computer. This isn't the first time Diego has waited until his mother is busy to express his wants or needs.

"I'm way behind on this report," Maria calls. "I can't take a break right now. You'll have to wait a few minutes."

"But Mom," Diego complains, "I'm really hungry." He continues to voice his requests loudly and insistently.

Maria repeats her pleas for him to wait, but Diego doesn't give up. Mom and Diego shout back and forth louder and louder, getting more and more irritated at each other. Finally, Maria barks in the loudest voice she can muster, "We DON'T YELL in this house!" Just as she realizes the complete contradiction in her words and the loudness of her voice, she hears Diego begin to whimper and cry. Clearly, communication, both verbal and nonverbal, has broken down.

What is needed at times like these is for parents to initiate what psychiatrist and author Daniel Siegel calls relationship "repair." Being securely attached does not mean misunderstandings and breakdowns in communication do not occur. On the contrary, they happen in the best of relationships. When miscommunications do occur, though, parents can turn them into learning situations. Here's what Diego's mother did.

DIEGO AND MARIA

✳ ✳ ✳

Diego's mother Maria takes a few deep breaths. She slowly walks downstairs, sits on the sofa next to her son, and says with a smile, "Let's you and me talk about what just happened."

"You yelled at me!" Diego shouts, anger written all over his face.

"You're right, I did," Maria says. "I lost my temper. That was my mistake. I said no yelling, but I was yelling. I guess we were both yelling, weren't we?"

"Yeah," Diego responds, and Maria can see the anger draining from his face and feel him calming down.

"Let's start over," she says. "How about next time you want to talk to me, you come to where you can see me and then talk in your nice, normal voice. That way neither of us will have to yell."

"Okay," Diego answers. "I guess I can do that."

"And now let's go look for some snacks you can get on your own when I am busy."

The repair for this conflict is now complete. Both mother and son have learned something. Maria is calm again, and she has provided Diego with alternative behaviors that will not be so upsetting to her.

PARENT SKILL BUILDER

Repairing a rift in your relationship with your preschooler

The ABCs of repair are Awareness, Breathing, and Correction.

Awareness: Harry Stack Sullivan suggested that awareness is necessary for change to occur; otherwise we are all doomed to repeat our relationship mistakes. Before you can repair, you have to be aware! It's so easy for parents to react automatically and unthinkingly to their children. Try to catch yourself doing this. The key to becoming aware of things you say or do that are not in your or your children's best interest lies primarily in the nonverbal realms. Pay special attention to facial expressions, postures, voice tone, and muscle tension that communicate negative emotions.

Breathing: Taking a few deep breaths can interrupt the negative physiological reaction that may be brewing. Perhaps your heart is pounding, your jaw is clenched, or you can feel tightness in your shoulders, chest, or stomach. Research in stress reduction shows that an effective way to interrupt this downward spiral is to take three deep "belly breaths"—inhalations so deep you can feel your abdomen expand, followed by slow exhalations. Take the time to do this, especially when you feel you don't have the time.

Correction: Once you are calmer, decide what you want to say or do to correct the situation. Maybe you decide to give your child a hug, maybe you decide to have a short talk about what both of you were feeling, or maybe you do both. Remember to avoid lecturing your child or explaining only your side. A good way to start is to ask your child, "What just happened here?" This allows your child to participate and thus builds self-esteem. It also conveys a positive message: "We can fix this."

Events could have taken a very different turn if Maria had decided to continue shouting, smacked her son in anger, or given him the cold shoulder. Or if she'd just gone back to work, hoping the whole thing would blow over. It certainly might have, but she would have missed a golden learning opportunity. Imagine if this pattern of blowing up, and then retreating kept happening in this relationship. The child would continually be left to try and make sense of his feelings all by himself. The mother would be setting a poor example for how to work with the feelings of frustration and anger that come up in any relationship.

Children need their parents to help them navigate the complicated ocean of feelings. It is helpful for them to see mom and dad appropriately expressing and working with their own feelings. Parents shouldn't fall into the trap of believing that they ought to always have it all together and experience and express only positive feelings. No one can feel and act positively all the time. The key is to use those times we make mistakes with our children as teaching moments.

The most important relationship skills children need to learn for negotiating with peers involve expressing and dealing with others' negative feelings. You can help your child develop these skills, not by showing perfect responses (in fact, that would be a disservice to your child) but by letting your child see you convey an attitude of friendliness and comfort toward your own feelings, negative and positive, along with a willingness to make mistakes and learn from them.

In the way Maria chose to handle the situation with Diego, the miscommunication was acknowledged and talked about openly. It only took a few words (young children generally don't respond well to long lectures). More important than the words was setting a certain appropriate nonverbal tone involving the use of voice and space. When Maria talked with her son, she sat next to him, at his level, and spoke calmly and gently. The nonverbal message was "We have time and we can fix this."

In getting along with others, nonverbal language may be just as important, or even more important, than words. When dealing with different emotional messages from both verbal and nonverbal channels, people tend to believe and respond more to the latter than to the former.

SPENDING TIME WITH YOUR CHILDREN

Finally, we want to emphasize the obvious: none of the suggestions we offer is more important than spending quality time with your child. We know how busy parents are, and how hard it can be to find time to be together. A main contributor to this lack of time is the pressure many parents feel to begin their children's formal education early, which results in many children leading highly scheduled lives at very young ages. A mother of a two-year-old lamented the fact that her daughter had missed the cutoff for preschool and would have to play in the backyard for another year. To make up for the educational opportunities she thought her daughter was going to miss, this mother scheduled extra art, music, and dance lessons for her daughter. Certainly, there is nothing wrong with children having some structured experiences outside the home, but in relationship terms, nothing replaces the simple act of parents spending time with their children, especially during the preschool years. Why? Because the best way for children to learn about relating is to relate to the adults to whom they are securely attached.

Remember that with young children, your presence and your attention matter. Nothing elaborate is needed. One of our children, at age four, called our time together the "time to see your eyes at me." Psychologists have discovered that what this four-year-old was expressing, in his own terms, is true. From the end of infancy until the beginning of the juvenile period is the time children learn basic verbal and nonverbal relationship skills through joint attention with their attachment adult—probably you.

To see joint attention in action, watch a mother or father with a child as the child deals with a novel situation. If you watch closely you will see them both observe the new situation or person. Next the child will offer a verbal label or a nonverbal behavior such as a facial expression or posture. Then the child and the parent will do something that is characteristically and wholly human—they'll turn and look at each other. During this joint attention time, the parent usually says or does something to confirm or reject the child's communication and offers a further explanation. This is where new words and concepts are learned and inappropriate ones are eliminated. Apes and monkeys can do many human-like activities. Even those raised as though they were human, however, cannot show joint attention.

Joint attention is an important process for learning during childhood, but joint attention cannot take place if one of the participants is missing. We urge you to spend time with your child so you can be her agent of learning and change. Joint attention interactions are really quite simple to set up. Face to face interactions might include playing together, becoming part of your child's pretend scenario, sitting outside and talking about whatever it is you see (trees, birds, cars, people walking by, etc.), or nighttime rituals (reading a story, talking about what was good about the day, etc.). Most parents realize that reading to their children is an excellent way to build and strengthen the parent-child relationship, but parents might not know that it is also important to have their children "read" to them (even before they can actually read). Children telling parents about what they think is happening on each page of a story has tremendous benefits, not only for stimulating intellectual growth but also for strengthening children's self-confidence and connection with parents.

Young children also enjoy side-by-side interactions, where parent and child are jointly engaged in a task. Many children love to be included in family routines and chores like shopping, fixing things around the house, watering plants, putting laundry in the washing machine, or raking leaves. Helping out with such tasks gives children a feeling of belonging and of contributing, which builds a sense of being valued and being part of this important first relationship. During these seemingly simple interactions, significant and lasting lessons can be learned about the give and take of relationships. While it's easy to overlook traditional, leisurely activities in our hyper-fast, competitive culture, the best education for children at this age is the slow and gentle education of interacting with people.

BREAKING THE CYCLE OF UNHEALTHY PARENTING

In some families, parenting styles or circumstances make it difficult for parents to provide what is needed for a healthy attachment.

GLEN

✳ ✳ ✳

Glen is a dad who believes there's not much to learn about being a parent. He comes from a "tough love" family himself, where children were to be seen but not heard. He feels that once you have a child, you automatically know what to do. If his children don't do what he says, they've "got it coming." He disciplines by using threats ("You don't eat your dinner and you don't play outside for a week"). His children are well behaved, but subdued, and they lack that

certain spark that preschoolers often have. Glen senses
this and, not knowing what's wrong, sometimes suddenly
demands, "Hey, what's wrong with you, son? Why are you
so quiet?" Not only are his children afraid of him, they
never quite know what to expect from him.

Like Glen, some adults have relationship difficulties that
make it hard for them to relate to their children in healthy ways.
Many parents had difficult childhoods. Sometimes these childhood struggles, which seem a long way off, are brought quickly
into the present when people have children of their own. Such
parents may find themselves relating to their children in destructive ways that echo their own negative early relationships with
their parents. It's an easy trap to fall into. How many times have
we caught ourselves saying or doing the very things we promised
ourselves we'd never say or do to our children?

CASSANDRA

✳ ✳ ✳

Cassandra is a mother whose own parents were not there
for her emotionally when she was young. Although the fam-
ily lived together, the parents spent a great deal of time in
their own world, oblivious to the needs of their children.
Now, this mother of two, not surprisingly, has a difficult
time when her children make emotional demands on her, as
young children inevitably do. Cassandra tries to be warm
and available, but more often than not she is sharply reject-
ing, with a get-out-of-my-face attitude. Because her chil-
dren can't depend on her for comfort and don't know what
to expect from her, they vacillate between sullen withdrawal
and intense acting out.

What should you do if you—like nearly half of all parents—had an insecure attachment relationship with your parents? The good news is that with awareness of your own strengths and weaknesses and some hard work, you can break the cycle of passing on to your children unhealthy patterns of relating.

First, you need to be aware when you are saying things to your children or acting in ways you know you don't want to. Sometimes keeping an interaction journal of what you did and how you felt about it is helpful. Enlisting the help of a coach is an excellent and proven way to improve. A trusted friend or family member who knows you well and is willing to give you honest feedback, especially concerning your nonverbal behaviors, could make a good coach. However, not everyone is comfortable enlisting the help of a friend or family member. Friends and family sometimes have a hard time being objective and family members, especially, may have come from the same unhealthy past. Another option would be engaging a professional counselor. A counselor is not only trained to provide the kinds of interpersonal feedback we have been talking about, but also has the advantage of being able to see you from an objective, unbiased viewpoint.

Second, you need to come to terms with your own childhood. This means being able to acknowledge and talk about it realistically—both the good aspects and the bad—with someone you trust. Mentally separating your childhood experiences from those of your children will allow you to say to yourself, "This is what my experiences with my parents were like. While some things worked, I know from my own feelings that there are some things I'd like to do differently with my own children."

You do not need to have a perfect childhood to be a good parent! In fact, understanding your own negative experiences will help you become more understanding of your children's feelings.

You need the ability and willingness, as an adult, to acknowledge realistically what felt right and what didn't in your own past. Then you need to be able to make a conscious decision—in that moment with your own children when things seem most difficult and you can feel yourself falling into a familiar negative rut—to do it differently.

Often, great harm is done when parents act in unhealthy ways without realizing it. But if parents can bring a gentle awareness and attention to being with their children, they have a real opportunity to change their patterns of relating. This takes lots of practice and patience—with yourself and your children. But it's something that pays great dividends in the parent-child relationship and in the child's relationships that follow.

If you become a better observer of your own behavior, especially your nonverbal behavior, your observations can give you valid information about how you are feeling and can help you relate more successfully with your children.

PARENT SKILL BUILDER

Increasing your awareness of how you interact with your child

Notice when you are feeling tense, because that is when you'll tend to resort to old, unhelpful ways of relating to your child. What are your tension signs? Do you clench your jaw, hunch your shoulders, furrow your brow, start breathing faster? Do you feel like your stomach is in knots? These physical signs are often a warning that you may be about to say or do something unhelpful. When you sense these signals, congratulate yourself! You've just taken an extremely important step in changing your behavior with your child. You've interrupted what could be a destructive pattern.

Stop whatever it is you were about to say or do and ask yourself,

"Is this really what I want to be doing right now? Is this really what I want to model for my child?" If this is not the path you want to be taking, give yourself some time to think about what it is you really want to say or do. Counting up to ten slowly is good. (And breathing deeply at the same time is even better.)

Decide your course of action and proceed. You'll be amazed at how quickly you can teach yourself to change your patterns.

Sometimes even good parents who are undergoing stressful situations may find that they have little left to give their children. This is especially true when parents feel isolated or overwhelmed and don't have much support from other adults. Raising children is an important, difficult job, and there is not a parent who doesn't need support and help from others at one time or another.

What kind of support? Well, parents need all kinds of physical and logistical help when children are young: someone to take the baby for a while or play with a young child while parents take a break, for example. Even more important is the availability of emotional support, the opportunity for mom and dad to seek advice from others or just to vent their feelings. A simple truth is that the more supported and cared for parents feel, the more likely they are to give the same support and care to their children.

PARENT SKILL BUILDER
Take care of yourself and your relationships

Here are some tips for taking care of yourself and your own relationships that will help you care better for yourself and help you relate better to your child.

Take some time for yourself. It doesn't have to be long—even a few minutes alone can be helpful. It's the act of doing it that matters. Have someone look after your child while you take a walk or jog, talk with a friend on the phone, read the paper or a chapter in a book, do some stretching or yoga, listen to music, meditate—anything that serves as a short break from the duties of parenting.

Give time to caring for the adult relationships that matter to you—your relatives, your friends, and, most of all, your spouse or partner. A phone call with a friend, a dinner out with your spouse, a few minutes at the end of the day to check in with your spouse about how you are both doing (see if you can do it without talking about the kids!) can make a big difference in having the energy you need to interact with your children.

Striving to make the attachment relationship work for you and your child will benefit your child's attempts to relate to others. Remember, this is a project in progress. You will always need to stay open to learning and discovering new insights.

Learning to relate through communication

A child's first attachment relationship sets the tone for future relationships. Children take what they learn from and through this early relationship as they navigate the complex demands of the peer and school world. Many psychologists believe children carry a blueprint of their first attachment relationship and use it to build relationships in adolescence and adulthood.

How does a healthy attachment relationship develop? No doubt you've heard the saying that real estate is all about "location, location, location." Well, for us, the making of a strong attachment relationship is all about communication, communication, communication.

Preparing for relationships outside the family requires learning about communication. As we've discussed in our other books about teaching nonverbal skills, effective communication depends on both verbal and nonverbal language competence. Children who are good communicators—positive in the way they express themselves with others and accurate in reading others' feelings and intentions—are more likely to be successful in relationships throughout their lives. These skills are learned primarily within the family and through the attachment relationship.

COMMUNICATING WITH WORDS

The words you use when you talk to children matter. Contrast these responses to two five-year-olds who have just broken open large bags of M&Ms and spilled them all over the floor. Amouri's mom says, "Oh, come on, Amouri, not again. How many times have I told you not to touch the candy? Why do you always make such a mess? Now just move out of the way while I clean it up." Contrast that with Antonio's mom, who responds: "Okay, Antonio, it looks like there's a mess on the floor. You know where the dustpan and broom are. Let me know when you've finished sweeping it up." In both situations, the mother acknowledges the spilled candy. But Antonio's mom's words offer a positive solution in which the child can participate. Instead of assailing her son's character, she simply describes what she sees and directs him toward a way to fix it.

Children whose parents talk to them realistically but positively, as Antonio's mother did, are able to make more and better friends. One reason is that children are great observers of their parents and will imitate the way their parents talk to them when they, in turn, talk to their own friends. Another reason is that if children receive positive responses at home, they bring that sensibility with them to the outside world. Being positive and generally agreeable verbally tends to elicit the same responses from others.

Children who feel and come across this way have happier, more satisfying relationships.

Another helpful type of parent-child verbal interaction is drawing the child out through the use of gentle questions. The process of drawing out a child appeals to the child's inner resources and encourages him to stretch his capabilities. It's like the way Fred Rogers, the late children's television host of *Mister Rogers' Neighborhood* used to talk to the children watching his show.

CODY AND HIS DAD
❈ ❈ ❈

Every day at the same time Cody and his father sit on the couch as Mister Rogers appears at the door to his house. As he calmly takes off his jacket and puts on his sweater, Mister Rogers sings his "Will you be my friend" song, which finishes with the words, "Would you be, could you be, please won't you be my neighbor?"

"Yes," Cody answers.

"Yes," his father echoes.

Then a short conversation takes place. Mister Rogers asks them how they are and they answer him. Mister Rogers tells them how pleased he is to be with them, and they respond that they are happy to see him.

Mr. Rogers taught us that you didn't have to be loud and strident to capture the attention of a child. Antonio's mother's approach to the spilled M&Ms was similarly calm and respectful, presenting both a problem and a way to take care of it.

Consider the case of three-and-a-half-year-old Sasha who doesn't want to share a toy with a peer in preschool. One way of handling this situation verbally might be to say, "Sasha, I can see that you want to ride on the tricycle right now. That's okay. But remember that Shaun would like to ride it, too. What can we do to make sure that Shaun also gets a turn?" This encourages Sasha to think about Shaun's desires as well as her own, and to think about possible solutions to the quandary of sharing (such as, "I will give it to Shaun when I am finished so he can have a turn, too"). Once again, the point is that children internalize language they hear from parents and use it not only when they talk to themselves, but later in their own friendships. Children who are spoken to respectfully and positively take these verbal habits with them into relationships outside the family.

Think of this as a Golden Rule of Relationships: Speak to your children as you would have them speak to you. And to others.

COMMUNICATING WITHOUT WORDS: READING AND SENDING NONVERBAL CUES

As important as words are to the relating process, their true meaning can be emphasized, neutralized, or even negated by nonverbal cues and behavior. Take this verbal message to a child: "Now that shirt looks good on you." If you say this with a smile and an appreciative look, your nonverbal cues are backing up your verbal message and the entire impact is positive. The child feels good hearing this. But what if you say the same thing with a roll of your eyes, a slow shake of your head, and a sarcastic tone? Will the child really believe what your words say? Not likely.

What if you use your voice to emphasize the second word as you utter the sentence? ("Now *that* shirt looks good on you.") What if you emphasize the last word? ("Now that shirt looks good on *you*.") Which message will leave the child feeling good?

Probably both, but the second message conveys (by emphasizing *you*) that there is something about the child that makes the shirt look great.

It pays for parents to be aware of how any verbal message is delivered. They need to be especially aware of the nonverbal messages they send themselves, but they also need to be good at reading their children's nonverbal cues. We'll consider each skill separately below.

It is especially important to be able to see things from a child's perspective when you are trying to understand the child's inner, emotional state. Children who have the frequent experience of "feeling felt," as psychiatrist Daniel Siegel puts it, also have the sense of being known and accepted for whatever their experience is. This sense of feeling understood translates into more effective ways of behaving with others.

The best way to understand a child's inner state is by being a good observer of what's not spoken directly with words. Children often do not or cannot put their feelings and inner experiences into words. (Neither, for that matter, do many adults.) Remember that an infant communicates with her mother nonverbally even before she is born through the rhythm of her mother's heartbeat. Children are better at nonverbal communication and depend on it more than their newfound facility with words. Adults need to learn how to look beyond surface behavior and words to appreciate what a child is feeling emotionally.

ALISHA

❈ ❈ ❈

Mother leads four-year-old Alisha into the first day of preschool. Holding her mother's hand tightly, Alisha lags a few steps behind and clutches a stuffed bunny to her chest.

As they enter the classroom, Alisha shrinks back from the noisy activity. Her face is pale and serious, her eyes wide. Her teacher, Ms. Lori, senses how tentative and scared Alisha feels. Lori quietly approaches Alisha and her mom. She kneels down in front of Alisha and very gently says, "Hi. You must be Alisha. I'm glad you're here." Huddling closer to her mother, Alisha says nothing. "This is a really big day for you, isn't it?" Lori says quietly. Then she smiles and extends her hand to Alisha. "Would you like to come with me and see your cubby? That's where you'll be putting that nice coat you have on."

Although Alisha says nothing verbally, she is communicating much nonverbally. Looking at Alisha's face and watching her movements and her proximity to her mother, Lori correctly guesses how frightening and overwhelming starting school is for this four-year-old. Suppose Lori misinterpreted Alisha's silence as comfort and either ignored or was oblivious to the little girl's signals of fear. Suppose she had rushed up to Alisha, saying in a booming voice, "Well, hello, there, young lady! What's the name of that cute little bunny? Here, let me have a look!" Imagine the distress this might have caused Alisha and how it might have colored her feelings toward beginning school.

Fortunately, Lori did read Alisha's nonverbal signals accurately, and she adapted her own nonverbal behavior, setting her rhythm to match Alisha's. (Remember that rhythm is the most basic and fundamental nonverbal channel, the one that sets and determines the general climate for all human interactions.) Effective parents and teachers are able to sense children's rhythm and to adapt their own, when necessary, to be in sync. Lori's nonverbal communications helped Alisha feel understood and accepted.

Being aware of your nonverbal messages can help you meet your child's needs.

PARENT SKILL BUILDER
Reading a child's rhythm

Have you watched an adult walking with a child? Have you noticed how, in many instances, it looks as though the child is being dragged along by the adult? You can almost see the furrows in the ground made by the child's shoes as he is pulled along. The two are out of rhythm.

Here's what we want you do: Practice matching your rhythm to your child's and see how that affects the way you relate to him. We think you will be pleased to see how much more relaxed and pleasant time with your child becomes.

Being a good communicator means being able to "get in sync" with what a child is going through, especially if strong emotions are involved. Most of us have witnessed situations where a well-meaning adult is out of sync with a child's mood and observed the resulting negative consequences. Consider these three scenarios:

STACEY
❊ ❊ ❊

Five-year-old Stacey is concentrating on copying the letters in her name. She leans over the table, biting her lower lip as she focuses on writing, ever so slowly, one letter at a time. Her mother, eager to connect with her daughter but not able to modulate her own rhythm and behavior to match Stacey's quiet focus, comes over. "What are you doing, honey?" she exclaims excitedly. "Oh, wow! Hey, want to come outside and play hide and seek with mommy?"

"Noooo," Stacey whines, agitated because she has been interrupted.

JOEY

❋ ❋ ❋

Joey, three and a half, is crying because he can't find his stuffed bear. In an attempt to help him feel better, his father ignores Joey's mood and picks him up and swings him through the air, saying, "Hey, it's Tarzan swinging from the vine! Wheeee!"

Feeling not only misunderstood but now angry, Joey screams to be let down.

JOMICA

❋ ❋ ❋

After months of trying, five-year-old Jomica has finally learned how to ride his bike without training wheels. He is thrilled. He runs into his house, bursting with excitement and ecstatic about telling his mother, who is talking with a friend. "Mom," he yells, "I did it! I rode my bike with just two wheels!"

"Jomica," his mother says as she frowns disapprovingly, "you are supposed to say 'excuse me' when you see that mommy is busy."

"Sorry. Excuse me," he says, less energetically.

"Now what did you want to tell me?" asks his mother.

Dejected, Jomica mutters, "Nothing," and turns to walk outside.

All parents misread their kids' nonverbal cues from time to time. It would be unrealistic to suggest that it's possible to make good connections with our children all the time. Problems develop when parents continually misread their children's signals or the impact they are having on them. What could Stacey's, Joey's, and Jomica's parents have done to be better attuned to their children? Let's take them one at a time.

Stacey's mother could have observed the intense concentration evident in her daughter's face and posture and decided to sit quietly next to her while she finished her letters. She might then have said, with quiet enthusiasm, "Wow, you worked very hard on those letters, didn't you?" If she wanted her daughter to go outside and play, she could have given her a little more time to enjoy her writing activity, and then said, "It would be fun to play hide and seek with you in the backyard. Let me know when you're ready."

Joey's dad failed to read his son correctly. He could have connected with his son's distress over misplacing the bear by kneeling down to Joey's level or gently reaching for his hand and saying softly, "You really need your bear right now, don't you? How about if the two of us look for it together?"

Jomica's mother could have recognized the importance of her son's accomplishment and decided to share in his obvious excitement, even if he was interrupting her, by saying with pride and excitement, "Oh, Jomica, that's wonderful! I'm so excited for you. I know how hard you've worked on riding your bike all by yourself." She could have discussed his interrupting behavior with him later, when she sensed that he was in a state of mind where he could really hear it.

What does it mean for children when their parents connect with them? Children whose parents respond empathically are more likely to develop a strong sense of self. Because the children are secure in who they are, they will have the psychological freedom to connect with others if they choose. In contrast, children whose signals are constantly missed or misinterpreted often find themselves caught up in internal struggles, with little energy left over to connect with others.

In the following two scenarios, we meet two children who are trying to connect with peers. The first child has the kind of self-confidence and easy ability to relate that is based in a secure attachment with parents. The other child struggles, not only with her sense of self, but with her ability to make contact with peers.

Amanda

* * *

A few girls on the school playground are playing jump rope. Seven-year-old Amanda would like to join the game. Amanda's parents are attuned to her inner states and adept at responding to her in ways that validate her experiences. Amanda approaches the game with curiosity and interest, confident that she will soon be included. At first, she simply watches, taking in the situation. Although she hasn't yet been invited to play, she takes on the energy of the girls in the game, laughing along with their fun and good-naturedly grimacing when they miss a step. She notices that one girl has been turning the rope for quite a while. During a moment when the girl accidentally drops the rope, Amanda calls out, "Do you want a chance to jump while I turn the rope?"

"Sure," comes the delighted reply. As the rope is turned over to Amanda, she now becomes a part of the game.

Stephanie

* * *

Stephanie, a girl whose parents are often out of sync with her, lacks self-confidence. Like Amanda, she wants to join the game of jump rope. However, unlike Amanda, she doesn't know what to do. She might hover timidly on the sideline, hoping to be asked in. Or perhaps she asks, in a whining, plaintive tone, to join the game. Or maybe, without first stopping to observe the situation, she leaps impulsively into the game and trips on the rope, to the exasperation of the girls already jumping. In any of these scenarios, Stephanie is not off to a good start with the other girls.

Amanda is fortunate. Her parents have given her a solid foundation in the skills of reading and responding to others' rhythms. We believe it is best if children learn to read social situations early through affirming interactions with their parents. But even if this early learning does not occur, parents and teachers can still help children improve.

UNDERSTANDING FEELINGS

Having satisfying relationships involves knowing about feelings. Think for a minute about your own close relationships. Odds are that when you think of someone who is close to you, you think of how that person makes you feel. This makes sense, because human relationships are built around emotion. In emotional learning, it helps if children are good at three things: knowing their own feelings, accepting those feelings, and being able to identify feelings in others. The skills are related: once you're aware and accepting of your own emotions, you are in a better position to recognize them in others.

How do children get comfortable with their own feelings? By having parents who, as psychologist John Gottman points out, convey an attitude of friendliness toward emotion. This does not mean consistently feeling or showing positive emotion; rather, it means being able to accept and work with whatever feelings come up. Here are two examples of mothers who are not accepting of their children's feelings.

JEANNIE

***

Six-year-old Jeannie has tears in her eyes. "I don't want to stay with the babysitter tonight," she says sadly.

Her mother responds, "Oh, come now, where did 'happy Jeannie' go? I want her back."

HEATHER

***

Heather, the same age as Jeannie, is crying over a broken toy. Her mother says, "Stop crying. You're fine. You're fine."

These two mothers, for their own reasons, are uncomfortable with unhappy feelings in their children. But by negating their children's natural experiences, they inadvertently teach that certain feelings are "bad" or not allowed. If they consistently respond to expressions of negative emotion this way, their children will have difficulty being close to others, because being in close relationships requires being comfortable with your own negative and positive feelings as well as those of others.

Young children who are on good terms with their own feelings are better off socially, so it pays to help children learn to be comfortable with their feelings, both negative and positive. Jeannie's mother could have said something like, "You seem sad, Jeannie. Let's talk about it." Heather's mother could have said, "I'm sorry your toy broke. I know how sad you feel. You really liked it, didn't you? Let's see if we can fix it together."

Being able to recognize feelings in others is another emotional ability that prepares children for healthy relationships.

Personality theorist Alfred Adler recognized this. He taught that a parent's job is to inspire what he called "social feeling" in children. To have social feeling means to care about the welfare of others. It is the ability to feel empathy, to be able to see and feel something from another's perspective. Children learn empathy when their parents talk to them about how others feel and think. For example, suppose a father and son witness a child crying during school drop-off. An emotionally attuned father could say to his son, "Tommy's crying, isn't he? What do you think he is sad about?" Or, alternatively, "Looks like Tommy's feeling sad about saying good-bye to his mom today. Maybe he needs a friend."

PARENT SKILL BUILDER
Helping your child become better attuned to others' feelings

One mark of a mature person is the ability to sense what others are feeling. You can nurture this ability in children by practicing three things:

Help the child "read" feelings through nonverbal cues. (Example: Direct the child's attention to another child's sad or angry face.)

Help the child put a name to the feeling the other person might be having. (Example: "See how Sheila has her head down and is walking slowly? Maybe she's feeling sad.")

Suggest to the child—in line with Adler's ideas—what that person might need right then. ("Maybe Sheila needs a friend," for example, or "Maybe Sheila needs a hug.")

In the quest for obtaining what we need from others in terms of caring, support, and love, we must learn how to communicate our own needs as well as how to recognize the needs of others. These skills are not innate and must be learned through interactions with our caretakers during childhood.

We now turn to an often neglected but nonetheless crucial situation where many critical relationship skills are learned—children's play.

Learning to relate through play

Young children depend on the attachment relationship to know that they are secure and valued, as well as to learn fundamental relationship skills. They begin using these new skills to interact with children (and with adults) at daycare, preschool, and play date settings.

SETTING THE STAGE FOR PLAY

Even when young children are spending more time with peers, mom and dad still exert a strong influence on how they behave. How so? For starters, parents decide with whom their child will interact. They exert a direct influence by selecting playmates and an indirect influence by selecting a preschool or early childhood program for their child to attend. Many parents interview directors and teachers at several preschools before choosing. The choice will likely be a place where parents of children attending the school will have backgrounds, interests, and values that are similar to their own. In this way, parents continue to exert their influence on their child's interactions.

Parents directly influence their children's play relationships by being close by to supervise and intervene if necessary, especially during playtime that occurs outside of preschool. (Children under five should not be left alone together for any length of time.) Young kids constantly seek out their parents during play. How many times have parents heard "Watch me jump!" "Look at me dance!" "Suksy won't share with me!" "They won't let me play with them!" or "Tommy kicked me in the leg!" Sound familiar?

When children play in a school setting, teachers are the supervisors. Adults strongly influence young children's relationships until children enter elementary school, when they begin to interact more with peers in isolation and form relationships on their own.

PRACTICING SOCIAL SKILLS THROUGH PLAY

What makes these early play relationships so important? First, while many preschoolers love interacting with other children and often refer to age-mates as "friends," the truth is that they are not yet capable of mature friendships. Rather, peer interactions in early childhood provide important practice for learning about how to get along with others, a skill that will be needed later when children are more on their own. As they play, children usually take what they have learned about interacting with others in the attachment relationship and try it out with age-mates.

Children's first attempts at interacting with others are sometimes unintentionally funny imitations of what they have internalized from relating to their parents. Take for example, a five-year-old who, in response to another child's invitation to play with blocks in the classroom, replied, "I'm sorry, I'm too busy for that. I have a report to do." It turns out that this little boy's mother was in the process of completing her college degree. No doubt, her son was imitating his mother as he attempted to relate to the other child.

Not only do children bring what they have learned from home into their early peer relationships, they also are quick to imitate each other—for better or for worse! Many parents have been surprised when a child uses a phrase or gesture that could only have been learned elsewhere. One young boy, upon hearing he was not allowed to watch a certain TV show, retorted in a voice dripping with indignity and sarcasm, "Fine," and stalked out of the room. As this response was not used by either of his parents, it was likely that he had picked it up at preschool. His teacher later confirmed this, saying that "fine" was a phrase that was going around the classroom, used with great relish by all.

CLEVELAND AND RAMAR

✳ ✳ ✳

Five-year-olds Cleveland and Ramar are on the play-ground during recess at their preschool.

Cleveland calls out to Ramar from the window of a large plastic playhouse. "Hey, Ramar, wanna come inside my dinosaur house?"

"Well, what's in that house?" asks Ramar.

"It's my dinosaurs and I'm feeding them lunch!" responds Cleveland. "Wanna help me?"

"Okay, but what kind of dinosaur is in there?"

"A giant T. rex!"

"Let's let him out!" says Ramar.

"No, no!" Cleveland shouts. "We have to feed him first. He's hungry!"

"Okay, I'm gonna bring the food. Hey, I need a big tractor to get all this food into the house! Vroooom... vroooom. Outta my way, everyone, I got food for a hungry T. rex!"

If you stop to observe almost any kind of peer interaction at this stage of development, you will find that it revolves around the magical world of play and make-believe. Unfortunately, imaginative play is in danger of becoming a lost art to many families. Developmental psychologists like Judy Dunne have pointed out the value of such play in exploring feelings and relationships. Other psychologists have cautioned that children whose play always takes place around toys rather than in their minds are missing terrific opportunities to learn more about themselves and about how to relate to others.

Unless parents intercede by providing too many toys, play comes naturally to preschoolers. Rare indeed is the young child who begins an interaction by saying something like, "Hello, my name is Nikkole. What's yours? Where do you live?" Watch carefully, and you will see that interactions at this age almost always begin with an invitation to engage in physical or pretend play. Often the interaction gets going even before the participants know each others' names.

LEARNING THE RULES OF PEER RELATIONSHIPS THROUGH PLAY

Play is where children learn the rules of peer relationships. Play teaches about relationships. Child educator David Elkind says play is "preparation for life." We argue that, along with the attachment relationship, play is preparation for *relationships in life*. What are children working on in early play relationships? For one, they are discovering and confirming that others have thoughts, feelings, and desires, and that the thoughts, feelings, and desires can be different from their own. Sometimes a hard lesson, this realization means that children must begin learning to balance their own desires with those of others—a major skill needed to relate to others successfully.

SOSHANA AND KAREN

✳ ✳ ✳

Soshana and Karen are almost four. They are playing "store." Karen is pushing a small plastic shopping cart while Soshana is putting items inside it. Picking up a small ball, Soshana says excitedly, "Let's pretend this is a coconut! I love coconuts!"

"That's too small," Karen responds. "Coconuts are much bigger, you know."

"Nooo, coconuts are NOT bigger than this ball," she says. "This is a coconut and that's IT."

"Is NOT a coconut," retorts Karen, beginning to whine.

"Is, TOO," says Soshana, sounding angry.

"Is not."

"Is, too." The retorts go back and forth, until one girl ends up in tears and parents intervene.

Soshana had a choice between asserting her own desires or trying to see things from Karen's perspective and maybe even trying it Karen's way. (No easy task for a young child!) In this case, Soshana insists that her view is correct and that the object in question must be a coconut.

Now imagine if one of the children—let's say Soshana—decided to change her response based on Karen's statement. Perhaps she's willing to try out Karen's way of seeing things. Here's how the interaction might go, after Karen states that the ball is too small to be a coconut.

SOSHANA AND KAREN

✳ ✳ ✳

"Um...okay, well...it's still round so it has to be something round," says Soshana. "I will make it a different kind

of fruit! I will make it a…an orange! A nice, round orange!"

"Okay, it's an orange!" says Karen. "Put it in the shopping basket. It's almost time to get home and make our lunch!"

One can imagine the two girls smiling at each other and walking off hand-in-hand. Of course, Karen could have shown a willingness to enter Soshana's world by agreeing that, yes, on their imaginary shopping trip the small ball could be a coconut.

The point is that this play interaction gave each child a chance, first, to try taking the other's perspective, and second, to use that knowledge to compromise. This involves trial-and-error learning. It's not unusual, especially when children are brand new at playing with age-mates, for first interactions to come to a stalemate.

Remember: Young children need to test the waters and make mistakes as they negotiate the new and sometimes confusing world of peer relationships. It's important that they get this chance to practice, as they will need the skill of seeing another's perspective once they enter elementary school.

As they play together, children also begin to learn and practice the skills of relationship negotiation. Any time two people interact, a kind of subtle "dance" occurs in which the participants decide, often unconsciously, who is in charge of the interaction and whether the encounter is friendly. As they play, preschool children are learning how this dance works by trying to negotiate. Through negotiation, they find out who is going to be in charge and whether the interaction is friendly or not. This negotiation dance becomes more important as children spend more and more time with peers (unsupervised by adults) in full-time school.

FOSTERING "GOOD" PLAY IN CHILDREN

How can play teach children about relating, and how can we foster good play so our children will learn? In any play situation, don't set your expectations too high. Remember that many young preschoolers are simply not yet capable of the kinds of relationship behavior shown by older children and adults. Preschoolers are just beginning to learn how to negotiate their way through the complex world of other people. Early play interactions are practice for what comes later. "Practice" means accepting the fact that mistakes will happen. Above all else, make sure that children's practice is FUN! Here are some helpful hints we've gleaned from parents and teachers.

Practicing Good Play

• **Arrange one-on-one play dates for your child.** From ages two to five, play dates are a great idea. It is best to begin with one child because it is often difficult for young kids to negotiate the complex demands of having more than one other child present. Consider one four-year-old girl's statement to her father: "Daddy, I switched friends today," implying that she can only have one friend at a time. Or consider a boy's reply to a classmate who invited him over for a play date: "I can't have a play date with you. I already have one with Tommy." What these statements reveal is that young children are not yet capable of handling the more complex behavior required when more than two kids are present (what to do, for example, when all three children have different ideas about how to play with a certain toy, or when two children are chummy together and a third gets left out). A child's best chance to practice new relationship skills is one-on-one.

- **Vary the structure of the play setting.** You don't need to provide a great deal of structure in the play setting. In other words, lead the children to the toys or to the playground and let them devise their own interaction. This not only fosters children's imaginations, but it also encourages them to take their own first, tentative steps toward relating to another child. Many children's interactions are now tightly structured by adults, probably much more than when today's parents were young. It's less common, these days, for children's birthday parties to take place in the family backyard, at a picnic table, with kids milling around the lawn or porch. Most birthday parties now are more likely to take place away from home in structured, adult-controlled settings (a bowling alley, indoor soccer field, craft store, or batting cage, for example). While there is nothing inherently wrong with a structured setting, it's a good idea for children also to have opportunities to make up their own play.

- **Provide opportunities for check-ins and check-outs.** Expect children to check in with you periodically and be ready to be asked to intervene. Young children can profit from adult guidance during their first interactions with peers. Balance your intervention so children get the adult help they need to learn but also have opportunities for appropriate practice to develop their own skills. Take the case of four-year-old Deanna, who seeks out her mother to complain about four-year-old Erlana, who Deanna claims is not letting her cook at the play stove. "Mommy, Erlana's not sharing the stove with me," goes the refrain. What should Deanna's mom do?

Let's start with what she should not do. Deanna's mom shouldn't rush into the room and scold Erlana for not sharing the stove. Deanna might temporarily feel that she has won the dispute because her mother has decreed she was in the right. But what has Deanna learned in this situation that will help her resolve future disputes with peers? Not much unless she can bring her mother with her to take care of all interaction difficulties.

And what about Erlana? She's likely to feel humiliated at having been scolded by Deanna's mom and may not want to play with Deanna again. While scolding may have alleviated the short-term problem, neither girl has learned anything useful about relating. Suppose Deanna's mom simply tells her daughter to "ask Erlana to share with you." What happens if Erlana says no? Again, neither child learns much.

Here's a way for Deanna's mom to approach the situation that might have better results. In a friendly, interested tone, she could say, "Oh, really? Hmmm. Let's see if we can all think of what to do together." Then she could walk into the room, sit down, look at both girls, and say in a calm voice, "Sometimes it's really hard for all of us to share, isn't it, especially when we really like what we are playing with." This way Deanna's mom is allowing both children to feel understood. It helps for both children to feel this way before they begin to compromise. Feeling understood prepares the groundwork for compromise to happen. Mom could continue, "Erlana, I see you're having a really good time with the stove. That's great. Can you tell Deanna when you are finished because she would really like a turn as well." Here, Deanna's mom shows that she realizes how much fun Erlana is having, but also suggests that Erlana will be able to turn the stove over to Deanna when she is ready. She gives Erlana a positive alternative to simply digging in her heels and refusing to let Deanna use the stove.

To Deanna, she might say, "Okay, Deanna, Erlana is going to let you have a turn as soon as she's finished. She's going to tell you when." This reassures Deanna that if she can be patient, her desire will be met. Once they are helped to see an alternative way of handling the situation, children are more likely to turn over a toy or share. The last bit of teaching here might involve having the children thank one another for compromising.

• **Act as a coach for relationship beginnings.** All relationships go through phases of choice, beginning, deepening, and ending. While preschool children are not yet sophisticated enough to understand that relationships have phases, there are some things adults can do to begin to introduce the idea, especially in the area of relationship beginnings. Beginnings of relationships are the most amenable to being taught.

One of our children attended a preschool where the teachers did a nice job of modeling manners and customs that go along with good beginnings. They greeted each of the children by name as they walked through the door in the morning. Children were gently taught how to make eye contact with the teacher when they came into the school, and how to greet with a handshake, a smile, and the words "good morning." Children quickly learned that these rituals were expected at school and were a necessary signal that the day was beginning.

Parents can encourage these good relating habits by modeling with their own behavior what they want their children to do. Children learn from watching the way you shake the hand of someone you've just met and say, "Nice to meet you." Learning is reinforced if you gently request that they do the same. Often, what it takes at first is saying the words yourself and then asking the child to repeat them. Most children of this age are happy to do this, as it makes them feel they are participating in an adult interaction. The key is to keep it simple and brief—no long lectures on manners!

Don't expect your child to be able to carry on an adult-length conversation yet. Often a brief "hello" or "good morning" is enough for young children, especially if they are interacting with adults. For example, if you and your child have just met a new young friend, you could say to your child, "Michelle, this is David. Let's have you give him a nice big hello." If Michelle says hi, smile at her and thank her for being so nice. It's a good lesson in developing positive habits of social interaction.

• **Coach playing on the playground.** Suppose Jessica is on the playground watching others play. She would like to become part of the play but doesn't quite know how to start. You can coach her by saying, "Jessica, why don't you go over there and say, 'Hi, my name is Jessica. Can I play with you?'" Sometimes all children need is the right words to help them start off on the right track.

We witnessed a mother do a nice job of helping her child strike up a conversation with another five-year-old on a trip to a children's museum. The museum was showing how balls of various shapes and sizes moved through the air differently. Kids could throw all kinds of balls into a big net and set off alarms and noises. This mom's son was having a good time throwing balls, but the mother noticed another boy standing on the sidelines, looking as if he didn't know how to join in. We watched as the mother called to her son, "Hayden, it looks like that boy would like to play. Why don't you go over and give him a ball and ask him if he'd like to throw balls with you?" Her son did exactly that, and the other boy appeared happy to be asked to play. This was a positive experience for both boys—not only the one who was asked to join in, but also the one whose mom coached him on how to invite someone else into an interaction. Both boys learned something about the skills involved in beginning a relationship.

PARENT SKILL BUILDER
Quick tips on setting the stage for good play

* Set up one-on-one play dates.

* Try to let children choose their own play. This is how they learn how to relate to other kids.

* Be ready for kids to tattle on one another at times. When this happens, don't take sides. Instead, help negotiate a compromise so both children feel their desires were at least partially met. For example, "Why don't you play George's game first, and ask George to let you know when he is ready to play your game." This suggests to both children that George will eventually let the other child have a turn.

* Remember to praise a child who is willing to wait her turn or who lets the other child decide what to play. Children need

to hear when they've successfully used a new skill, especially when they have shown self-control.

* When on the playground, if your child needs help joining in, provide a few simple words to help start off the interaction.

REPAIRING PROBLEMS IN CHILDREN'S PLAY SKILLS

Play is important because it lets children practice skills they will need later, when they begin to develop their first real friendships. The practice they get at this age helps. Research shows that children who are more skilled at interacting with peers are better liked and better adjusted overall. This does not mean that preschoolers must start out with perfect social skills—they are expected to make mistakes. But what if they seem to have trouble developing play skills? How can you tell when a child is having difficulty, and what can you do to help?

Josh is a five-year-old boy who wants to play with others but seems hesitant to ask another child to play. He often watches other children longingly as they mill about the playground, immersed in pretend games. When his mom says to him, "Why don't you go play with the other kids, honey?" he shrinks back and clings to his mother, as if afraid to venture out into the world of other children. For children like Josh, this skill doesn't come naturally, but it is an area in which a little extra coaching can go a long way.

The first thing Josh's mom might consider is organizing a one-on-one play date, so Josh will have a ready-made playmate instead of having to choose someone amid the din of the pre-school classroom or the playground. One-on-one play dates can be less intimidating for young children who are hesitant to strike up relationships. Josh may be more inclined to play comfortably with one child, especially if the play date is at Josh's house, where he is on familiar territory. Sometimes it's also helpful for a child like Josh to play with a younger child. Playing with someone younger can build social confidence in the older child and provide a nice opportunity to stretch the abilities of the younger child.

Suppose that Josh and his mom happen to be on the playground, watching kids run around. Josh's mom might help him spot a child playing alone to approach. The key here is for Josh and his mom to watch the child for a few minutes to get a sense of what the child is doing. Entering an interaction works best when a child first watches and gets the lay of the land; the parent can then help the child extend the play. For example, if the child is on the jungle gym pretending that it's a rocket, Josh's mom could suggest that Josh tell the child he's bringing some "rocket fuel" to make the rocket go higher.

Remember that there is a chance the invitation will be rejected. It's not unusual for young kids to reject an attempt by a peer to enter into a play situation. Sometimes this is done quite directly, as in "No, I don't want to play with you!" When that happens, it's important to reassure your child. "That's okay. I guess he really wants to play by himself right now. But you did a good job of asking to play with him. Let's find something else for you to do." Kids need praise for their efforts, even—especially—when those efforts are not successful.

What's next?

Throughout childhood, children are under the protective dome of parental love and guidance. If all goes well, children will have learned much about how to make relationships work, first through interactions with their parents and then with their peers under the watchful eyes of their parents.

The relationships children face as they begin full-time school are different from those that characterized their infancy and preschool days. Children must now learn how to relate to other children as equals, away from adult control. This is a large and important step, and children often stumble and fall as they pursue relationship success. Parents took care of them after the falls they experienced in their infancy and childhood, but now parents can step back and view their children's fumbles and mistakes as wonderful opportunities for conveying lasting relationship lessons and hope that their children internalize these lessons.

At this stage children must be able to pick themselves up, learn what they did wrong, and try again to relate to their young peers. Much is riding on the success of these early attempts to practice their relationship skills, not the least of which is a happy and satisfying adult life. As we'll see next in the juvenile stage, children will now take what they've learned in this phase—for better or worse—as they enter school and begin to navigate the complex world of peers.

What is to be accomplished by the end of the childhood stage?

- To deepen the attachment relationship with parents
- To deepen a healthy sense of self and an appreciation of others' feelings
- To develop skills needed to relate to others, especially peers

CHAPTER V

The Juvenile Stage
(Five to Ten Years)

✳

Learning to make friends among peers

Establishing a healthy sense of control

What a child should learn during the juvenile stage for forming healthy relationships:

- To make same-age, same-sex friends outside the family
- To understand that others have minds of their own, and have thoughts and desires that may not match theirs
- To understand how much of what happens to them is under their control

Much happens during a child's first five years of life. No longer a helpless infant or a blundering toddler, a five-year-old is now a young girl or boy who is ready to become a fully functioning equal partner with peers. Children prepare for this new stage by learning about themselves and others primarily through the attachment relationship with their parents. Because most children have been in a preschool or have had play dates, they have tested the relationship waters by practicing their accumulating social skills with their peers under the watchful eyes of parents and teachers. While children may differ from one another in the level of relationship skills they have attained, what most of them have in common is the parental presence that governs and guides their interpersonal interactions. Whether through setting up play dates, choosing a preschool, or supervising playtime with friends, parents set the tone for children's beginning attempts at friendships during infancy and childhood.

All this changes now, as children embark on what will be, for most of them, about thirteen years of full-time schooling. The major change on the relationship front is the presence, importance, and influence of peers. The cozy and circumscribed interactions with parents and with children chosen by parents, now expands to include people who are same-age (and adult) strangers to them and to their parents. While parents certainly continue to be important in their children's lives, they now share their influence with others. At the juvenile stage, children spend more than half their waking life in school and with playmates in outside activities.

A child now trades a familiar home situation in which she has been the center of attention in a small group of familiar adults (and perhaps siblings) for a school setting where she is one of many children who are, at first, strangers to one another. Entry into this new world of peers is often difficult. To negotiate this transition successfully, children will need help and support from caring adults. Because children spend less time at home now, how time is spent there becomes even more important for continued learning about relationships from parents.

This challenging transition is also a wonderful opportunity for growth. Since we believe that human beings are born with an innate drive toward psychological health, even if children have experienced relationship difficulties at home, their natural tendency toward growth can make use of the school situation as a **corrective learning experience**. In other words, what might have been broken interpersonally earlier in life can be fixed through school experiences. Because of this corrective possibility, the school community can become the most important non-family interpersonal environment in a child's life.

Learning to make friends among peers

Learning how to form **co-equal** relationships with peers (or, more simply, learning how to make friends) is the single most important social emotional goal for children of elementary school age. Developing peer relationships is a uniquely different process from developing relationships with adults. Peer relationships provide opportunities for kids to learn about themselves in ways that adult-child relationships cannot provide, and they require different skills and ways of being. If children succeed at learning to form peer relationships, they will have a big head start in becoming happy, satisfied adults.

If all goes well, children will end their elementary school years able to relate to peers as a group, and they will have acquired what Harry Stack Sullivan called a "chum" and what we call a true "best friend." Though parents and children are bound to one another in nurturance and caring, it is through the chum relationship that children expand the meaning of trust and love to include someone who is a peer and equal to them. "Chum love" means putting the wants and needs of a peer ahead of your own, and it is an important development in the juvenile stage.

AUSTIN

✳ ✳ ✳

It's a warm, breezy September morning and the first day of school for the third graders at Osborn Hill Elementary School. On the playground during recess, there is a constant buzz of energy as children mill about. Teachers stand by, arms folded, and talk amongst themselves. Some children are having a contest to see who can swing the highest. Others hang upside down on the monkey bars, and still others stand in groups chattering excitedly. Over by the playground fence, ten-year-old Austin huddles in a group of five or six boys, as they bend over to examine the latest baseball cards.

"Oh, man, you're so lucky! You got my favorite hitter!" *Austin exclaims as Yestro produces a card.* "Man, I've been looking all over for that one. That is so cool!" *Austin gazes appreciatively at the card while Yestro proudly displays it for all to see.*

"Hey, you want to trade that one? I'll give you three of my classic cards for it," *Austin offers.*

"Nah, I want to keep it for now," *comes the reply.*

"Yeah, okay, I'd keep it too, if I had it." *Austin smiles.* "Well, if you ever want to trade it, can you give me first dibs on it?"

"Sure, I'll come to you first," *says Yestro.*

Austin looks up as another boy jostles into the group. "Hey, Yannick, did your dad take you to the doubleheader last night? Did you get to see the grand slam?"

AVA

✳ ✳ ✳

Over on the other side of the playground, ten-year-old Ava stands with a small group of girls under the monkey bars as they giggle and compare their new shoes. "Oh, my mom got me the exact same shoes except they're the lace-up kind, not the pull-ons," *Ava says excitedly to Chante.* "Those look so good on you!"

"Thanks," *Chante replies proudly.*

"Hey, can somebody spot me?" *asks a redheaded girl who is swinging from bar to bar.*

"Sure, Gina," says Ava. "How about I spot you and then you spot me, okay? How fast can you go?" Ava stands near Gina to help her if she slips. "Terrific job. You're really good. Okay, my turn!"

For their age, both Austin and Ava are skilled at relating. Because they are comfortable with themselves and at ease with others, their age-mates want to be around them. They also share interpersonal skills that are characteristic of socially well-adjusted elementary-school-age children. Both show an **enthusiasm** about what they are doing that is contagious to others, yet is not over-bearing or off-putting. Both children are **flexible** and **creative** when it comes to negotiating. Austin demonstrated this skill when he noticed Yestro didn't want to trade cards yet; Ava did likewise when she suggested taking turns spotting her friend on the monkey bars. Both listen well and extend themselves to others, as Austin did when he told his friend how lucky he was to have a good card and as Ava did when she admired her friend's shoes. Neither is relegated to the sidelines, yet neither demands to constantly be the center of attention. They both convey interest in others not only with their words but, more importantly, with nonverbal behaviors like facial expressions and tones of voice.

As we explained at the beginning of this book, relationships go through a series of predictable stages, starting with **choice,** moving on to **beginning** to get to know a person, and then **deepening** the relationship into a friendship over time. Finally, children must learn how to **end** relationships positively. Through an appropriate ending, they become aware of what they did right and what they did wrong in the relationship, and they use this new knowledge to begin new relationships.

Unlike younger children whose parents direct most of their activities, school-age children need to learn to navigate these more adult-like steps with their peers on their own. Although it is difficult at times, parents should stay more in the background of juvenile relationships than they did earlier. Ideally, by the end of elementary school, children will have learned how to successfully negotiate the relationship process. An important point to remember is that, contrary to what many people think, friendships in childhood (and in adulthood, for that matter) do not just happen by accident. They are the result of learned skills, lots of opportunity to practice, and trial and error. Most kids who are good at relationships have accomplished that goal by working at it and getting better and better with practice and with guidance from parents and teachers.

The choice phase. All relationships start with a choice.

GAIL

✳ ✳ ✳

Eight-year-old Gail has just moved to a new school. It's lunch hour during her first day. Her classmates have descended on the lunchroom, and the hall that was quiet a moment ago now reverberates with the sounds of chattering voices and chairs scraping against the floor as children get seated at tables. Gail stands holding her lunch box and watching the scene as her peers choose tables.

What does Gail do now?

Before she even thinks about where she wants to sit and what to say, she first has to have a desire to interact. For most children, the decision to interact is easy because they want to relate to their peers. By the time they are in school, and often long before that, children show a natural intense interest in other kids their own age. However, for a small minority of children who want to relate, the decision to interact with peers is painfully difficult, a decision fraught with such anxiety and dread that some choose not to relate at all. Other children choose not to relate to peers because they don't want to interact with anyone. The loss of any desire to interact with others usually characterizes children who suffer from conditions such as depression, schizophrenia, and autism—conditions that can cause them to withdraw into private, inner worlds. Children with one of these diagnoses need more help than this book provides. They need serious psychological intervention to develop an interest in social activities or (if they have social interest) to remove the impediments that prevent them from initiating contact with others.

Most children, however, desire to relate to someone their own age, and the immediate problem they have to solve is choosing the person with whom they will begin.

GAIL

✳ ✳ ✳

Gail looks around the crowded room and sees a lot happening. One group of boys is laughing uproariously over the fact that one of them has blown air into his empty chips bag and hit it hard, causing a loud pop. At another table, several girls sit up very straight on the edge of their chairs, drinking from juice boxes and swinging their legs back and forth under the table. Each wears a skirt with matching sandals and sports a ponytail. Gail spots another table where boys sit at one end and girls at the other. Although they are with their own "groups," they occasionally trade barbs back and forth. A girl in jeans and a T-shirt calls one of the boys "really, really annoying" after he squirts punch out of his mouth. A few children are still in the lunch line, and still others are milling around deciding where to sit.

To whom does Gail gravitate? With whom will she ultimately decide to chance an interaction?

Psychologists know that when Gail makes this decision, she will do so quickly, based on information she has picked up nonverbally. When starting a relationship, we choose people who make us feel at ease and comfortable and who are like us. Like most other children her age, Gail will choose to be with others of the same gender. (This phenomenon doesn't begin to change until the end of the juvenile stage and the beginning of early adolescence.) Gail will probably also look for girls whose clothes and hairstyles are similar to hers.

How does Gail tell, without knowing or speaking to any of these children, which group would present the best possibilities for friendship? To make her decision, Gail will observe their **nonverbal behaviors**—facial expressions, tones of voice, postures, gestures, clothing, and hairstyles. Will she be drawn to the ponytailed girls swinging their legs back and forth? To the few loudly trading insults with the boys? Or to someone she has yet to notice?

Gail glances around—it is important to know that this all takes place in a matter of seconds—and wonders, "Who looks inviting? Which kids might I have something in common with? Who is likely to accept me?" Gail's decision of where to sit is based on an astonishingly quick, nonverbal reading of the different scenes in front of her. If her choice is based on an incorrect reading of the situation, then the chances of her initial interaction moving forward successfully are not good. If her choice is based on sound observations and an accurate reading of what is going on, then she can move to the next phase of the process and begin a relationship.

The beginning phase. It helps to get off to a good start.

GAIL
❋ ❋ ❋

As Gail surveys the scene in the lunchroom, she wonders anxiously whom to choose. Her gaze focuses on a group of girls who are just beginning to sit down. As they take their places, one of the girls pulls a macramé friendship bracelet out of her lunch box and holds it up proudly. It's a colorful weave of red, blue, and yellow cords. Two of the girls exclaim over it as they admire the pattern. Gail feels a flutter of excitement, as she also loves to make friendship bracelets. Maybe she has something in common with these girls! Inside, she is nervous. Her stomach is doing flips. She has never spoken to them before. How will they respond to her? Will they be friendly? Taking a deep breath, Gail pushes through her scared feelings and walks bravely over to the table. She catches the eye of the girl with the bracelet and smiles.

"Hi, I'm Gail, I just moved here. Can I sit with you?"

"Yeah, sure," says the girl, smiling broadly. "I'm Jessica, this is Annie, and this is Chantal."

"Hi, guys. Thanks." Gail smiles again. "I was standing over there and I saw your friendship bracelet. I really like the colors. Did you make it?"

"Yeah, I just finished it and I was going to give it to Annie—"

"But now she likes it so much she's keeping it herself!"

interrupts Chantal, and all four girls giggle.

"Have you seen the one with the candy stripe colors?"
Gail asks. "I think it's so cool."

"Oooh, that's exactly the one I wanted to try next,"
chimes in Chantal.

"Yeah, that's the one I wanted to try, too. Want to work
on them together sometime?" Gail offers.

"Sure," replies Chantal, "How about I ask my mom if
you can all come over my house tomorrow, and we can work
on our bracelets together!"

Exchanges like this one, where children make their opening contact with each other, are so important. It is now, during what psychologists call the beginning phase of the relationship process, that children lay the groundwork for developing their first real friendships. Real friendships start with shared experience. On a deeper level, they involve the ability to show genuine interest in and concern for the other person as well as a way to share one's own feelings.

Gail's situation provides some direction about what we need to learn to begin a relationship. We learn that we should first introduce ourselves and then make "small talk." Gail also knew how to establish common ground by bringing up the friendship bracelet. Just as important as contributing to or initiating an interaction is the ability to listen to what others are saying, not only in words but also in the language of nonverbal cues. If Gail is to be successful, she will pay special attention to and make sense of others' faces, voice tones, and body language and send her own nonverbal cues effectively.

In successful beginnings a child respects the flow of a conversation while finding a way to become a part of it. Parents may have helped teach such skills earlier, but now for the first time, a child is attempting to accomplish this without parents or teachers to help if things go badly. Gail manages to do this well and comes away from her first contact with an invitation to another girl's house—a sure sign of success.

On another somewhat deeper level, children must wrestle, as Gail did, with the universal human wish to be accepted. Who among us cannot remember a time when we longed to become part of a group that was just out of our reach or when we felt the pain of being rejected by someone with whom we badly wanted to be friends? It's important to note that not all beginning efforts automatically result in friendship. In fact, at this age, all children, no matter how skilled or socially savvy they are, will experience more than an occasional rejection. Unlike adults, who may have enough experience to know how to behave tactfully in social exchanges, children at the juvenile stage can be quite blunt and to-the-point, as in the case of a boy who was overheard to say to another boy, "You smell. Get out of here." It's important for children to develop resilience in the face of inevitable social rejections and, most importantly, *to learn from them*. That is where consistent encouragement and support of parents and teachers are so important.

As a parent, the first thing to do is to listen to your child and empathize with her feelings. The temptation for many parents is to jump in immediately and offer advice. This is a normal urge. It is very hard for parents to see their children hurting. Offering advice may seem to be the best way of trying to fix the problem quickly and make the pain go away. But when kids who have been through a difficult situation are asked what adult behaviors were most helpful to them, the vast majority say "listening to me."

Simply listening may be enough to help a rejected child feel better. At other times you may need to engage in a little gentle problem solving. Problem solving is generally most effective when it's phrased in the form of questions that help a child think through a situation. Psychologist Lawrence Cohen suggests the following three questions: "What did you try?" "How did it work?" and "What might you do differently next time?"

Parents can also help by making sure that children have more than one context in which to socialize with peers. If a child is experiencing rejection on the playing field, for example, it can help to give the child a chance to interact with others in a completely different context—a scouting group, perhaps, or an afternoon club.

To make friends, children need to be good at beginnings. This is something all children can learn.

JAKE

* * *

Eight-year old Jake has just started summer day camp. It's a nature camp with participants from all over the local county. Jake is the only one attending from his school, so he does not yet know any of the other children. After introducing Jake to his counselor, mom waves goodbye and gets in her car. As she drives away, Jake surveys the scene in front of him. There are lots of children waiting for camp to begin. Some are by themselves, others are paired off, and still others cluster in groups. Jake's eye catches a group of three boys who are crouched down, examining something on the ground. One boy picks up a stick and appears to be prodding something gently. Curious, Jake walks over to see what they are looking at. As he approaches, he sees that the boys have located a giant beetle. He remains standing, watching the huge bug and listening to the others as they discuss it.

"Get back, Kobe, that thing could bite you!" the second boy warns.

"Nooo," responds Kobe authoritatively. "These things don't bite people. My dad told me. They just eat other, smaller bugs."

"Turn him over with the stick!" says the third boy. "I want to count all his legs!"

"Okay, I'm just going to do it softly because I don't want to hurt him," says Kobe.

As Kobe gently turns the beetle on its back, Jake crouches down next to the boys. "Wow," he exclaims. "That thing is huge! Where'd you find it?"

"Crawling right across the parking lot, over there," Kobe responds. "I didn't want it to get run over by a car."

"He's lucky you saved him," says Jake.

"Yeah, he could have gotten crushed by a tire, you know?"

There is silence as the four boys contemplate the beetle, which Kobe has now turned upside down on the ground.

Jake breaks the silence. "Once I was watching Jeff Corwin on Animal Planet, and he found the biggest beetle in the world, the "Goliath" beetle. He weighed it and it was a quarter pound!"

"Oh, wow," says Kobe. "That's way bigger than this one."

"Yeah, I think he found it in Africa," says Jake. "And know what? While he was talking about it and he was on TV and everything, the Goliath jumped right onto his face and he couldn't get it off and he was yelling and screaming!"

"Ewwww, gross!" comes the collective, appreciative response. All four boys start laughing at Jake's imitation of

Jeff Corwin trying to get the world's biggest beetle off his face.

"I love that guy," says Kobe. "He finds the coolest stuff, like that time he rescued that python snake in the fishing shack in Indonesia!"

"Oh, yeah, I saw that one," says the third boy.

"Hey, you guys want to walk together and look for stuff in the woods today?" Jake ventures.

"Yeah, let's be a group!" says Kobe.

ALI AND LISA

✳ ✳ ✳

Ten-year-old Ali is attending the same camp for the first time. She says goodbye to her dad and, as he drives off, she stands in the parking lot, hugging her backpack and looking around. Like Jake, she doesn't know any of the kids. Most of them are boys. As she looks around, she spots a girl about her age with a knapsack on her back, waiting for camp to begin. She, too, is watching the others. She looks friendly.

Ali decides to talk to her. As Ali approaches, she smiles at the girl. Her smile is returned immediately. "Hi, I'm Ali. Are you doing nature camp, too?"

"Hi, I'm Lisa. Yeah, with all these boys," Lisa says as she laughs and rolls her eyes.

"Oh, I know, there's hardly any girls here!" exclaims Ali. "I really like science so I begged my parents to let me do this camp. But none of my friends wanted to do it with me."

"I know," says Lisa. "A lot of girls I know are doing gymnastics camp. But I want to be a biologist and so I'd rather do this."

"Wow, that's cool that you came not knowing anyone either," Ali responds appreciatively.

"Yeah, I just hope it's good." Lisa giggles. "How come you decided on this camp?" she asks Ali.

"Oh, I love my science teacher, and I want to teach science someday. She told my mom about this camp."

"Oh, I like my science teacher, too," says Lisa. "He's kind of weird sometimes, but he makes the class really fun." Both girls laugh. "Want to walk together on the hike today?"

"Sure," Ali responds, delighted to be asked.

Jake, Ali, and Lisa are good at beginnings. Reading about their first day at camp could give you the impression that beginning relationships is easy. It's usually not. Beginning well takes skill and work.

How children can begin relationships

• **Use powers of observation.** Both Jake and Ali relied on their powers of observation before making contact with others. Both are eager to get to know other children, but before jumping in, they watch and listen to get the lay of the land. Others' nonverbal behavior is a key source of information about their attitudes and feelings—things most people don't put into words. For example, suppose a child has a scowl on his face. This usually is a good sign that beginning with him might not work out. Observation skills can be coached and practiced. Parents can model effective ways of getting information from watching people.

Research shows that kids who are skilled at beginnings and, in particular, at entering groups are adept at observing others before interacting with them. What do they watch and listen for? For starters, before breaking in on a group, they pause to get to know what the group is doing. They try to get a sense of what the members are talking about, what kind of rhythm the group has (are the kids talking fast, are they energized, are there pauses in the conversation, are there interruptions?), and whether the group seems friendly and open to taking in another member.

Before Jake says anything to the other boys, he stands back and waits until he has a sense of what the boys are talking about and how they feel about the topic—and about each other. It's clear to Jake from his observations that the boys are interested in the same kinds of things he is. Moreover, since they are sharing what they know about beetles, there is a good possibility they might be interested in hearing about the topic from someone else.

In the case of the girls, Ali notices that Lisa is standing by herself, doing much the same thing she is doing, and that the expression on Lisa's face is open and friendly. Ali also notices that the smile she gives Lisa as she walks over to her is returned warmly, another nonverbal signal that Lisa is open to an interaction. If Ali observed that Lisa had her back turned to the other kids or looked angry, sad, or uninterested, her decision about whether or not to approach Lisa might have been different.

It's very important for kids to be aware that they can continue to use their powers of observation once they have made contact and the conversation has started. Mel Levine, a psychiatrist and advocate for learning-disabled children, has termed this being the "friendship sleuth," and it is something that can be practiced and coached.

• **Wait for the right moment.** Maybe the biggest mistake kids make at the beginning of meeting other kids is coming on too strong or forcing themselves into the interaction too soon. It is all about close observation and good timing. Think about what might have happened, for example, if Lisa had looked angry and Ali had missed this important cue and approached expecting to be welcomed? While it's certainly possible that Ali's approach might have caused a positive shift in Lisa's mood, the girl's angry face might have meant that she wanted to be left alone. If that had been the case, Ali might have been rebuked for her efforts to be friendly and not known why.

Or suppose that Jake had not taken the time to get a sense of what the boys were talking about and launched, instead, into a story about his favorite toy car? Our guess is that the other boys would have ignored him or perhaps even told him to go away. Even if they tolerated him just to be polite, it's unlikely that he'd be invited to be part of their group on the nature hike. What Jake does that helps get things going interpersonally is to add to the conversation in a way that acknowledges the other boys' contributions but also advances the conversation.

• **Avoid hovering.** At some point, it's important to move from observing to interacting. Kids who have difficulty with beginnings often seem stuck at watching. They hover perpetually on the sidelines but never really initiate interaction or become part of what's going on. Suppose Jake had approached the boys, but instead of crouching down beside them and eventually chiming in on the conversation, had just stood there watching them. It's unlikely that the other boys (especially at this age) would have invited to him to get in on the action. In fact, after a while his hovering behavior might have been perceived as weird or annoying.

Or imagine if Ali had walked in Lisa's direction but just stood nearby looking at the trees, or staring at Lisa without saying anything. Lisa would have probably felt uncomfortable and might have walked away.

It's important to have the skills to move from observation to action, to be able to move beyond watching and walk up to a person or a group and introduce oneself, make a statement, or ask a question. The skill of "making small talk" is a necessary aspect of beginning any relationship. In a peer relationship, it is up to the children themselves to make small talk. At this age, there will not always be an adult nearby to get things rolling for them.

To help a child who has difficulty with beginnings, parents can try role-playing games in which the parent takes turns being the one who approaches and the one who is being approached.

• **Use icebreaker questions.** A good way to start an interaction is to ask a question. Jake, Ali, and Lisa all do this as they are making contact with new kids. "Beginning friendly" questions are easily answerable, pleasant in tone, and move a conversation forward. Examples of helpful icebreakers:

"Hi, I'm Gina, what's your name?"
"Want to play/study/work together?"
"Which class are you in?"
"Who's your favorite teacher?"
"Where do you live?"

Questions like these show interest in the other person, and they pave the way for a conversation to begin.

• **Ask the right sort of questions.** Not all questions are alike. It's important to ask questions that are not hostile or confrontational, and that don't call attention to personal or physical characteristics. Examples of questions not to ask at first:

"Why do you have that big mole on your neck?"
"How come you have to wear glasses?"

"How come you can't run fast?"

"Are your parents divorced?"

For obvious reasons, questions like these can be interaction killers. Sometimes children have to be reminded that it's one thing to think thoughts like these but it's quite another thing to say them. When we are getting to know another person, some things are better left unsaid. Later in a relationship, after you know someone well and are in the deepening phase, is the time for more personal questions and statements.

• **Show interest in others.** Jake, Lisa, and Ali all show interest in the kids they are meeting. This is also true of Gail, Ava, and Austin in the earlier scenarios. None of these children monopolizes the conversation by talking endlessly about themselves or only about what interests them; they are all good at appreciating what others are saying.

Jake, for example, asks the boys where they found the beetle and is impressed with the fact that they "saved" it from the parking lot. Ali shows appreciation of the fact that Lisa came to camp not knowing anyone, and Lisa, in turn, is curious about what made Ali come to camp. Similarly, in the lunchroom Gail shows interest in the girls' friendship bracelets.

• **Take turns in conversation.** Sometimes kids who are not afraid of striking up conversations with others still run into problems because they talk exclusively about themselves or about the one thing that interests them. Certain children find it very difficult to stop this behavior even though they are aware of it and told by others to stop. Many children diagnosed with Asperger's disorder have this deficit, and it prevents them from successfully interacting with peers.

In any interaction between two people, turn taking is crucial. For any interaction to start off well, there has to be give-and-take among participants. Children don't like it when one person monopolizes a conversation and is oblivious to the reactions of others. For example, imagine the irritation the boys might have felt if Jake had come up to the group and immediately starting lecturing them about what beetles eat. It would be one thing if he did this as an already established member of the group, but quite another if he launched into a monologue the first time he met the others.

It is important to understand that behavior that is appropriate later in a relationship can be inappropriate early on. If Jake had monopolized the conversation at the beginning before he knew the other boys, we can imagine them rolling their eyes at the know-it-all who has interrupted their discussion. Jake, instead, does the interpersonally astute thing of simply listening to the boys' conversation about beetles.

Later, when Jake tells the story about the Goliath beetle, it's important to note that he has waited to make his contribution until he has a sense of how the boys interact with each other. And then, rather than contradict or argue with anything that has been said, he offers a funny anecdote. Of course, there are times when it is perfectly appropriate to disagree. In fact, this happens all the time among friends. However, the very beginning of a relationship is generally not the time to launch an argument. Disagreements are less difficult to manage in later phases of a relationship when kids are on more solid ground with each other.

• **Find common ground.** Remember that the whole purpose of beginning a relationship with others is to see if continuing it is worth the effort. To this end, relationship beginnings often go more smoothly if kids find that they have an interest or an experience in common. When this happens, the conversation tends to flow more easily.

Children who are good at beginnings are often adept at finding out what they have common with others. Gail sees that the girls at the lunch table have a friendship bracelet and knows this is an interest she shares with them. Right away, she's got something to talk about that the other girls will likely be interested in. Although Ali knows nothing about Lisa, she knows that they are both in the same situation—starting the first day of a camp full of boys. She uses this topic as a way start a conversation with Lisa. The girls then go on to discover that they both love science.

• **Be aware of others' nonverbal signals.** Children can talk too much about themselves, and they can just plain talk too much. Even if others are interested in a topic, they will quickly get bored if they have no chance to contribute to the conversation. Often loquacious children are unable or unwilling to slow down and read the nonverbal responses of others. If they did, they might note signs of disinterest, such as looking away. Some children will come right out and say that they are "bored" or that someone is "talking too much," but most of the time these feelings are shown nonverbally, with facial expressions (by looking bored or irritated) or postures (by turning away from the speaker). To be socially successful, a child must be adept at reading and sending nonverbal cues.

• **Be positive.** Children who are generally upbeat, who seem to enjoy what they are doing, and who seem interested in the people around them have better relationships and higher self-esteem. In fact, research shows that the single best indicator of popular children is that they smile a great deal of the time. And all of this is tied in part to skill in nonverbal communication. Researchers successfully used an intervention program to improve the ability of eight-year-olds to read emotion in facial expressions. Children met in small groups once a week for thirty minutes. They were directly taught to **discriminate**, **identify**, **express**, and **apply** nonverbal information. After five weeks of training, the children's ability to use nonverbal information increased from below to above average for their age and so did their self-esteem.

Even though the single best predictor of how accepted and how popular children will be is *how much they smile*, even children who smile a lot have negative feelings from time to time—they feel angry, sad, hurt, disappointed, or just plain grouchy. Because everyone occasionally has feelings like these, it's important to help children learn to accept such emotions and work with them. The following suggestions may make the task easier.

Help children identify and name the emotion. For example, "It sounds like you are feeling sad (disappointed, angry, hurt, or the like)."

Convey that it is okay to feel this way. Negative feelings pass away much more quickly when they are allowed to be present for a time. When parents send the message that it is okay to feel angry, for example, it is much easier for children to let the anger go. Often when children get the message that it is not okay to have their painful feelings, they get stuck and continue to struggle with their emotions.

Ask if there is anything you can do to help at that moment. Suggest something specific: "Would a hug help?" or "Would it help if we went on a short walk together?"

However, the simple truth is that relationships get off to a better start when kids act and feel positive about what they are doing. Imagine, for example, if Ali had approached Lisa by saying,

"This camp is going to stink. My mom made me come and I know I'm going to hate it." It's possible that, if Lisa had similar feelings, she might relate to what Ali is saying. But that's a big gamble for Ali to take, given that she knows nothing about Lisa. Lisa is more likely to respond by thinking, *Wow, this girl is a downer. I sure hope she's not in my group on the nature hike.*

Similarly, what if Jake had come up to the boys watching the beetle and said, "Ew, that's disgusting, crush him!" or "That's just a stupid beetle. I've seen millions of them." Imagine the response from the boys who are obviously interested. "What goes around comes around," is very true in relationships. Being positive pulls positive responses from others. It's contagious.

Where are parents while children are getting relationships started? Parents should now become coaches, guides, and cheerleaders. They should offer support, but stay more in the background than they did when their children were younger.

PARENT SKILL BUILDER
Helping children with beginnings

* **Show interest in children's friendships.** The important thing here is to make sure that your interest does not become intrusive. Avoid being the prosecutor. Don't bombard your child with questions, especially if she is reluctant to give details. More important than finding out every detail of your child's friendships is the ability to convey that you are open, available, and interested, should she want to talk. In the long run, you'll find out more this way.

* **Accept and empathize with children's feelings, especially negative ones.** "It must hurt not to be invited to the

party." Or, "I'm sorry he made you mad. Do you want to talk about it?"

* **If your child seems stuck about what to do, invite him to solve the problem by asking open-ended questions.** Doing this helps children to articulate their options, and that's very empowering. "Is there something you'd like to say to him?" or "Have you had any thoughts about how you'd like to handle that?" or "Is there someone else you'd like to invite over to the house?"

Generally though, parents need to back off a bit and give children room to learn how to relate to equals. As they go through this process, children will make mistakes. Parents who see difficulties should resist taking over and should, instead, give their energy and support to their children's attempts to relate. Unless there are significant problems, too much control can be a serious mistake. *Children must learn on their own how to deal with their peers.* Like learning to walk, the process will be characterized by stumbles and falls. Parents can't walk for their children, and they can't relate for them.

Teresa Bolick, a nationally recognized expert in childhood development, says that children can gather "social capital" through their interactions. Every time a child succeeds at a social encounter, he makes a deposit into his "relationship account" that can be used to offset future social failures and errors. She offers this example: A boy with Asperger's disorder makes a social blunder. On a separate occasion, the most popular boy in the class makes the very same social mistake. Other kids ridicule the child with Asperger's disorder, but they ignore the popular boy's error, primarily because the former has little or no social capital in his relationship account while the latter has plenty. Your job as a parent is to help your child accumulate social capital on his own. He won't get a medal if you win a footrace for him; he won't accumulate social capital if you interact for him.

Children need parents to be more like guides and coaches than controllers. Children have much to learn about the way that relationships operate, and parents have much to teach. At this stage, the trick for mom and dad is to find ways to support healthy relationship development in their kids without over-orchestrating or dominating this important new aspect of their kids' lives.

Suggestions for coaching children on how to begin relationships

• **Find ways to model relating with others.** You as a parent can guide and coach your children by finding times and places to interact with them as you'd like to see them interact with others. We do not suggest that you give up having final authority about important things in your children's lives, but we do urge you to find times and places to model the way that co-equal relationships operate. You can do this by allowing your children to observe the way you interact with other adults and then talking about what went on. Or you can practice giving your son or daughter experience interacting with you as an equal about where to go, what to do, and what to talk about.

To be sure, there are strong biological imperatives that drive people toward one another. At the most basic level this might even be seen as the instinct that two are safer than one out there in the real world. Many of us are familiar with the work of Robert Fulghum (the author of *All I Really Needed to Know I Learned in Kindergarten*) who suggested we "Always hold hands when crossing the street." There would be no hand to hold if we had not established a relationship! In this sense, as well as in many others, relationships are fundamental.

• **Plan mealtimes at home with your kids as often as you can.** Where and how do children learn to translate this basic need to connect with others into real relationships? Books, TV, movies, and music? Sure. Watching friends? Probably. However, the prime sources of information and modeling for children are their parents and immediate families. We know this because research shows that kids who have better relationships with others and are better adjusted socially and psychologically come from families that have certain habits and characteristics. The children in these families not only have more and stronger relationships, but they also do better in school, are less likely to get into serious trouble, and are more resilient in the face of adversity. What's their secret?

These families *have dinner together more than three times a week!* But before you rush out to the supermarket, be aware that it is not the food that matters. When people sit together and eat, they talk. And when they talk, they share stories about their day's experiences, recall family memories and legends, and discuss times with special relatives and friends. They talk about problems and how they were solved or can be solved. They tell of good times and of bad times. In the long run, these family conversations provide a basic foundation for living in the social world that children cannot get anywhere else.

Research shows that the most frequently discussed topics during family dinners concern interpersonal issues. These discussions show children that relationships are important. Further, the task of maintaining relationships is modeled as children hear parents talk about their friends and see their parents as people with relational activities and time commitments. Finally, as the family builds its own unique history—the family narrative—children see that friendships are second only to family in importance. They learn that people are more important than cars, houses, electronic gadgets, and designer clothing.

PARENT SKILL BUILDER
Modeling relationships during mealtimes

✻ Banish the TV, the cell phones, and the iPod.

✻ Establish an explicit rule that everyone gets a turn and that everyone is expected to talk, including parents.

✻ Avoid falling into a pattern where the children are the only ones talking about their day. Though they certainly benefit from sharing their stories, a more important lesson to learn is about reciprocity in relationships. Children must learn to be good listeners as well as good talkers. Children learn valuable relationship lessons—patience, empathy, attentiveness—by hearing Mom and Dad talk about their own daily lives.

✻ Model listening, problem solving, and caring about others by your own behavior.

• **Enlist older family members to help you coach your children.** Another source of relationship knowledge is the family stories that children hear. In this case, the input of the grandparents—most notably the grandmothers, the people whom anthropologists refer to as the "kinkeepers"—is crucial. Kinkeepers are the people who tell children the stories of their families. They tell about troubles the children's parents faced when they were young and how they solved them. They tell of relationships that transcend generations, connections between people and families that go back well beyond the years of the child's life. They tell of times that were good and times that were hard. The stories are of triumph and failure, but they have one thing in common. Children typically hear them in the safety and warmth of stable homes that exist despite what the stories convey. The big message is this: "Lots of things—good and bad—happen to families and to people. But look, we are okay. Things work out; connections with people survive. Connections help us survive—they'll help you survive."

Armed with knowledge of their family's history, children develop what is known as an intergenerational self. This is a sense that they are larger than themselves, that they are part of a chain of people that stretches back decades, even centuries. They learn that they are never really alone, but carry with them traditions, knowledge, and wisdom that have been gathered over generations and that belong to them. With these treasures in hand, they are stronger and more capable socially and will be more successful in relating to others.

- **Offer to be helpful as your children interact with peers.** As your children's coach and guide, it is okay for you to find a private time to comment on the ways they interact with their peers. However, even if it is obvious, do not lead with criticism about what they did wrong. Instead, show your children you are watching and paying attention by first pointing out what they are doing right. We'd ask you to follow the *one-in-five rule* here: For every criticism you make, offer at least four positives. Researchers have found that people who are happy receive more than four times as many positives as negatives in their lives. Children, as do we, thrive on hearing about what they've done well. This is especially true when children are having trouble meeting kids or beginning relationships with others.

Keep on the lookout for even the smallest elements of competent relationship behavior and comment on them:

"I noticed how you gave that girl a big smile. That must have made her feel good."

"I heard from your teacher that you asked the new boy to sit at your table at lunch. What a nice thing that was to do."

"I saw what a nice handshake you gave your mom's new friend. I bet that made her feel really welcome in our house."

"I noticed how well you listened when your brother was talking. You made him feel important by listening the way you did."

• **Be aware of how you interact with your children.** The secure attachment relationship with parents that was the vehicle for children's learning about their world as infants and toddlers remains an important resource for children to tap now that they are in full-time school. Children hear *what* you say about them, but even more they listen to *how* you say it (it's those "nonverbals" again). You as a parent can help your children by working at becoming more aware of how you interact with them. It is easy to imagine that Jake (the boy who made friends quickly at day camp) grew up securely attached to his parents in a home where he was listened to, respected, and made to feel like he mattered. The positive messages he received from his parents go into the self he is becoming and show up in the ways he treats others. The same will be true of your child.

The deepening phase. We began this book by saying, "Beyond hearing that a child is doing well in school, few things make a parent's heart leap more for joy than to hear that a child 'has friends.'" To make real friends, to form friendships that can stand the test of time, children must be able to go from being with other children simply for playing games to being involved with them in a deeper, more meaningful way.

Choice and beginning, though important, are comparatively simple parts of the relationship process that most children can accomplish with practice and guidance. Since good beginnings increase the likelihood that friendships will follow, children who are poor at beginnings will face an uphill battle when they try to deepen their relationships with others. Attempting to deepen a relationship so that it becomes a friendship is more difficult and demanding than beginning one.

Similarity governs most of the choices about beginning a relationship. At the choice and beginning stages, similarity in age, attitudes, personality, size, intelligence level, activities, and physical maturity affect decisions about the people with whom we interact. This is consistent with the saying, "Birds of a feather flock together." However, during the deepening phase, a new principle of relating becomes important, illustrated by the phrase, "Opposites attract." You may wonder how these two different ways of thinking about relationships have remained valid for so long. The answer is simple: Both are correct.

When we attempt to deepen a relationship, everything gets more complex because in friends we seek *a mixture of similarity and difference*. Most of the activities of the deepening phase of relationship are calculated to help us first to find and then to relate to those who we later will find out complement us. This idea is captured by what is called the **circumplex.** According to the circumplex model (see figure below) the ways we interact

DOMINANCE

Hostile Dominant		Friendly Dominant

HOSTILE ———————————————————— FRIENDLY

Hostile Submissive		Friendly Submissive

SUBMISSION

with others can be described by two independent characteristics: **affiliation** and **status**.

Affiliation refers to the type and intensity of feelings we have for other people, which can range from hostile to friendly. Affiliation operates on the principle of **similarity**; if you are friendly you will (most likely) get friendliness in return, and if you are hostile you will (most likely) get hostility back.

Status, on the other hand, has to do with who is in charge of a relationship. It operates on the principle of **opposites** and is anchored at one end by **dominance** and at the other by **submission**. If you are submissive, you are likely to pull others to be dominant. If you are dominant, you will most likely pull others to be submissive.

Because status and affiliation are independent characteristics of relating, they can be crossed with one another to form the four major interpersonal styles that are shown in the diagram on page 161: **friendly dominant**, **friendly submissive**, **hostile dominant**, and **hostile submissive**.

The friendly dominant person leads in an open, pleasant, and helpful manner. He or she is usually the first one to speak up and offer to guide, help, or otherwise give advice. A classroom teacher or the captain of a sports team might favor this style of relating.

Friendly submissive persons are ready with a smile to follow the directions of others, whether in a classroom or on the playground. While they are not eager to lead, they feel very comfortable working with others who do.

In contrast to friendly dominant individuals who lead by affability, hostile dominant people lead by boldness and aggression. Hostile dominant individuals do not suffer fools gladly and are not afraid to demand that others comply with their efforts to lead. Individuals with this style of interaction are most comfortable in competitive situations where efforts must be maximized to achieve a goal quickly.

Hostile submissive individuals are most comfortable interacting with someone who will tell them what do in a straightforward, no-questions-asked manner. Again, this style of interaction is most prevalent in competitive interactions.

We may favor one interpersonal style over the other three in our interactions, but if we are well adjusted, we are able to use any of the styles, should the situation call for it.

The circumplex model helps explain what takes place during the deepening phase. Research has shown that when we move from acquaintance to friendship, we look for someone who is similar to us on affiliation and opposite to us on status. For example, if our interpersonal style is friendly dominant then we are searching for someone who will be friendly submissive. A friendly dominant–friendly submissive pairing is a **complementary** relationship, one that is a good candidate for a lasting friendship.

Before starting elementary school, children's complementary relationships are usually dictated by their parents and most often take place with the parents present. In these interactions, parents are dominant and children are submissive; if the relationship is a good one, then the feeling tone is friendly. When children begin elementary school, however, they start to relate to peers in relationships where neither status nor affiliation is determined ahead of time. Because relationships among peers (unlike those with parents) are between equal partners, social information has to be obtained and given out so that children can negotiate interpersonal styles—who will be dominant or submissive and whether the interaction will generally be friendly or hostile.

Once **complementarity** is present, then **reciprocity** can be developed. Reciprocity is a true give-and-take that includes **self-disclosure** and **mutual understanding**. You can see that this is serious business compared to the interactions of preschoolers. Real friendship during the juvenile stage, if attained, must be nurtured by both participants and has implied obligations for each of them. As deepening continues, trust grows. Accomplishing this takes time and practice, and the lessons learned will be applied for the rest of a child's life.

JAMIE AND NARABI

✳ ✳ ✳

Jamie has been sitting at lunch with three other boys for the first few days of school. They all look somewhat alike in the clothes they wear and eat similar lunches, but Jamie already likes Narabi better than the other boys. When the guys play at recess, Narabi usually takes charge of the game, suggesting what to do and who is to be positioned where. He's nice about it. A couple of times he has complimented Jamie on his playing. The two other boys aren't as happy with Narabi as Jamie is. They often argue about what other games to play or what roles they should have. After recess, Jamie and Narabi frequently separate from the other boys and walk back to class together, sometimes hitting and pushing each other playfully.

What Jamie and Narabi are doing is moving out of the beginning part of a relationship and testing to see if a more serious friendship is possible. So far it appears that a complementary relationship is developing, with both boys friendly, Narabi dominant, and Jamie submissive. Time and nonverbal communication skills will play important roles in whether the relationship stagnates, ends, or deepens.

From the perspective of deepening a friendship, choosing to spend our time with people and giving them a lot of our time are powerful ways of showing how important they are to us. Children need to be able to understand the meaning of time cues sent by peers and to express their own time cues appropriately. In the first instance, children need to learn how to pick up relevant cues from others that indicate whether they do or do not want to spend time with them. For example, if a child knows that a peer has to meet his mother after school to go to the doctor, then that child should recognize that this is not the time to ask to play a game.

Children also need to learn to send accurate time cues of their own that reflect how busy they are. Friends shouldn't keep you waiting if you have let them know that you are in a hurry; to make others wait communicates a lack of care or interest.

BEN

✳ ✳ ✳

Ben and his playmates are getting ready to play ball. He asks them to wait for him while he goes home to get his glove. While he searches for his glove, he turns on the television. He becomes interested in the program and watches it until the end. Twenty minutes later he runs out of his house to find that his playmates have gone on without him.

Time cues are significant indicators regarding status and affiliation. Most children learn the importance of time cues by experiencing the angry or hurt feelings of disappointed playmates. Children who fail to pick up time cues must be taught about them directly. Time cues help children decide whether or not to try and deepen their relationships into friendships. Jamie and

Narabi's time together is providing them with an opportunity to get to know each other. Up to this point, there is agreement about being friendly, and there is negotiation about who will be dominant and who will be submissive. At the moment, it appears that they both are comfortable with Narabi leading and Jamie following. Only time will tell if a true friendship will develop.

How can parents help? Once again we suggest guidance rather than direct control. Research shows that children left to their own devices will most often work out their social interaction problems effectively among themselves without adult intervention. But besides letting children take their relationship lumps, parents and teachers also can help by providing appropriate social opportunities for children to interact with one another. At times, this seems counterintuitive. Adults, especially teachers, are more likely to spend more time figuring out how to separate children than looking for ways to get them to interact more effectively. Harry Stack Sullivan believed that the single most important goal of the juvenile stage of development is learning how to make friends. He criticized American society for putting so many impediments in the way of children learning how to get to know one another better. Nowhere was this more evident, Sullivan believed, than in the classroom, where, in the guise of maintaining order and discipline, attempts by children to connect with one another are often frustrated and punished. He suggested that academic and social goals could be more effectively met if teachers and parents understood the importance of peer friendship formation and made it more a part of the learning process.

LEXI AND BELLE

✻ ✻ ✻

Lexi and Belle are friendly with one another, and their talk sometimes disrupts class. Ms. Withers, their teacher, cautions them to pay more attention to their work and less attention to each other, but to no avail. One day Ms. Withers calls the two girls to her desk and tells them that she's concerned about their talking. Rather than split them up to prevent the disruptive behavior, though, Ms. Withers tells Lexi and Belle that if they promise to be quiet, they can work together on a project at the end of the day. The girls readily accept this offer. Over the next few weeks, the girls keep their part of the contract by being quiet during class because they know they can talk when they work on the class project at the end of the day.

Lexi and Belle's teacher came up with a solution that worked out her classroom difficulties, facilitated academic learning through cooperation, and encouraged the budding friendship. School is a place where children learn many lessons, but none is more important than learning to make friends; teachers should help them in meeting this goal whenever possible.

Nonverbal communication plays a significant role in the strengthening of relationships. Long before words of friendship are spoken, children communicate a deepening friendship through a continuous, meaningful, and reciprocal stream of nonverbal behavior. Facial expressions are one obvious indicator of a relationship's process. Other, more subtle nonverbal cues that reflect the ongoing state of a relationship are **personal space** and **touching**.

As relationships deepen, personal space usually shrinks between participants. Jamie and Narabi showed this, for example, in the way they walked side by side into school and in the way they separated and distanced themselves from other peers by their physical closeness to one another. As they headed toward the school doors, they also showed their shared potential friendship by the use of touch that is characteristic of boys—they playfully punched and shoved each other. For girls, friendliness also is shown by reduced physical space and touching, but the touching in their case usually consists of pats and hugs.

More subtle and less noticeable, but potentially as important, are nonverbal cues like **rhythm**, **paralanguage**, **postures**, **gestures**, and **objectics**. All convey emotions that reflect whether relationships are deepening, stagnating, or ending. Watch children who are becoming friends. They walk, talk, and act more in rhythm with one another as their relationship becomes more positive and deepens. In fact, it is difficult to know if complementarity between peers leads to similar rhythms or vice versa, but we do know that when both complementarity and similar rhythms are present there is a freer flow of information and an increasing chance that the friendship will flourish.

Rhythm is part of paralanguage as well. The speed and inflection of the human voice creates a kind of emotional music that must be read and expressed accurately for children to get to know each other better. Children must also be able to pick up emotional cues in others' tone and intensity of voice—and send those kinds of cues correctly—if they are going to make friends.

Ironically, some children have more trouble communicating nonverbally with peers than they do with adults. For example, research on children who are oppositional or who have other behavior problems reveals that while they have no difficulty identifying emotion in the tone of voice of adults, they have considerable trouble telling if children's voices are sad, usually misreading them as angry. It is easy to see how such mistakes could lead to acting out because misperceiving someone as angry when they are sad means you are likely to see him or her as a threat rather than someone who needs help—a sure recipe for social trouble.

Postures and gestures share subtlety with rhythm and para-language. A reliable indicator that children's relationships are moving in a positive direction is that their gestures and postures *mirror* one another's. Children who are becoming friends will move their hands, stand, and walk alike.

A person's posture is an important way of communicating status in an ongoing interaction. Even though children deepening a friendship will share similar postures and gestures, they also will use them to communicate who is in charge and who is supposed to be following. Children who fail to show postures consistent with their feelings or who don't accurately pick up the postural cues of others will soon be in interpersonal trouble. Researchers have found that children who are socially anxious have significant difficulty reading or sending postural and gestural cues of anger. This suggests children are socially anxious partly because their inability to read or send anger cues accurately in their postures and gestures causes interactions with peers to fail. Frequent failure would make anyone anxious about future interactions.

Objectics—what we communicate by our clothing, hair-styles, jewelry, and the like—become much more significant for children in the juvenile stage. Image at this age is all-important; wearing the wrong clothes or shoes can have a devastating effect on a child's ability to get along with peers. Children who hang around together will often dress alike. It is one sure way to show they belong and have friends.

Parents can gently guide children to make sure they don't become too extreme in their objectics, but parents also have to be careful not to force their own ideas of what is stylish on their children. This is especially true when parents want their juvenile age children to dress as though they were still in the childhood stage. Parents will have to step in, though, when children attempt to dress too provocatively, as though they were in the adolescent stage, which is yet to come. During the juvenile stage, parents and children must perform a delicate balancing act in sharing power and making decisions. (For additional information on nonverbal aspects of communication please consult the list of books in the back of the book.)

The ending phase. For many reasons, some friendships will come to an end. And, just as there are optimal ways of beginning and deepening friendships, there are skills to be learned and applied in ending them. Remember that a major benefit of ending relationships successfully is being able to look back and identify what was done right and what was done wrong. What children learn from a past relationship can be applied to making better new relationships. However, ending relationships positively is not that easy, and the truth is that we all have problems here. Rather than objectively reviewing what we've done in our relationships as we should, we (and our children) often avoid thinking about how we have handled the endings of our past relationships. Sometimes we allow a friendship to fizzle out by getting very busy and spending less and less time with the other person. Other times we become angry and upset about something the friend does or says and let that be the excuse for letting the friendship drop. Such actions may make ending easier to tolerate, but they prevent us from becoming aware of our part in making the relationship end negatively.

Knowing how to successfully accomplish endings of day-to-day interactions and events is a skill that can be applied to the endings that occur at the end of longer and deeper relationships. Preschool children generally don't handle any type of ending well, and this example gives a quick lesson in how *not* to do it.

JIMMY AND EDGAR

✵ ✵ ✵

Preschoolers Jimmy and Edgar are on the floor playing with trucks. Back and forth the trucks go over imaginary roads, hills, and valleys. The boys laugh and make engine noises. Jimmy's mother comes to the door and says, "Jimmy, it's time to go home. Say goodbye to Edgar."

"I don't want to go!" Jimmy yells.

"Say goodbye," Mother says more firmly. "Now!"

Jimmy stands up, throws down his truck so that it crashes into Edgar, and shouts, "I don't want to play any more anyway! Edgar is just stupid!"

Elementary-school-age children need to move on from the often-impulsive endings of childhood to more thoughtful and helpful ones appropriate for their stage of development. To help guide them on their journey of discovery, adults—especially their parents and teachers—need to function as coaches who model appropriate behavior, then teach and reinforce it. An excellent way for children to learn about endings is by watching adults end appropriately.

When a relationship interaction is over, say something nice about your time with the other person. An adult may say how good the food was or how much he enjoyed talking about a particular topic. A child may say she had fun playing video games or exploring the woods. The important point is not what is said, but that something is said to indicate the time spent was good.

Remind children when an event will end, so they won't be surprised when time is up. This is true both for relatively brief interactions that might take place during a single hour, afternoon, or day, and for relatively long-term relationships that might last over a summer camp experience or a school year. Teachers and camp counselors or other adults who are with children for defined time periods can be very helpful in making endings work better if they make the children aware of how much time is left before the end. That gives children the chance to do what they want to do and time to review what they've done with one another before saying goodbye. In many schools teachers post signs or make posters in their classrooms showing the number of days remaining in the year to remind students of when their relationships will end. As the end of the school year draws near, teachers can help children complete history timelines to remember the important events that occurred over the year. This is useful in making children aware of what they enjoyed and what they didn't, and what role they might have played in determining these outcomes. A timeline can be a terrific tool for learning about relationships because it makes public to all relevant parties what went into the relationship from its beginning to its ending.

Use rituals and transitional objects to mark endings. In his book *From Beginning to End: The Rituals of Our Lives*, Robert Fulghum describes rituals as the "cairns" marking the path behind us and ahead of us. For example, most children have bedtime rituals that mark the end of the day. Perhaps they are given a certain time at which they must put away what they are doing, wash and change into pajamas, and then read, listen to music, or do something else before going to bed. Most of the time for younger children, parents are part of the ritual whether it is reading a story or saying prayers. Children become very good "quality control experts" concerning bedtime rituals and will point out when some activity was left out or not done as well as it should be. Only when the rituals are done can children end their day and go to sleep so they can begin a new day in the morning.

Ongoing relationships also deserve rituals to mark their endings. One of us teaches a seminar on relationships to seniors who will be graduating at the end of the semester. There is much academic work in the course, but one of the most important elements of learning is experiential. The students are challenged to end their college relationships so that they learn what they did right and what they did wrong over the past four years of relating to others. In this process they often remember and reconnect with people from various places and times in their college experience and let them know how they played a part in their college years.

In addition, one of the goals of the seminar is coming up with a way of marking the end of our class. This is not as easy as it sounds and we spend considerable time thinking of how to accomplish that. Although the endings differ they are similar in the fact that they all involve creating a public ritual marked by transitional objects. One year, we decided to make a "yearbook" with all of our photos and short biographies. At the end of another year we mixed and poured cement into which each of us embedded one item that had personal meaning to us. In fact, that rather unrefined monument remains a permanent structure in the front yard of the professor who taught that seminar.

Juvenile stage relationships are the first ones that children have entered into on their own terms and when they end them they should be marked by personal ritual and transitional objects. Perhaps your children already have pieces of cloth, a rock, or some other piece of physical evidence of school, camp, or religious settings that signaled the importance of some past relationship. Our guess is that these are usually kept in a disorganized fashion in some drawer, but do not let their apparent disuse fool you. They are important. Just try and throw them away and you will find out how important they are.

Just as children need reminding that school or camp or an overnight is coming to an end, children should be encouraged and taught to come up with ways to mark the ending. And it is important at this stage of development that adults give children freedom to come up with their own choices.

Toward the end of the juvenile stage, a child will be poised to experience a unique relationship with a same-sex peer. This type of friendship, called the **"chum" relationship** by Harry Stack Sullivan and "best friend" by us, provides a template for the important relationships to come. This is how Sullivan described what he meant by a chum.

> If you will look very closely at one of your children when he (or she) finally finds a chum…you will discover something very different in the relationship— namely, that your child begins to develop a new sensitivity to what matters to another person. And this is not in the sense of "what should I do to get what I want," but instead "what should I do to contribute to the happiness or to support the prestige and feeling of worth-whileness of my chum." This change represents the beginning of something very like full-blown… love.

Do you remember having a childhood chum? Whenever we ask this question at our relationship workshops, most everyone says yes. When we ask workshop participants to describe their best friends, the descriptions are very positive. With smiles on their faces, participants tell us how wonderful their chums were and how they spent countless hours talking with them in person and on the phone. Their fondest memories usually include how comfortable and secure they felt in the company of their special friend, and how much they trusted and were trusted in return.

The ability to acquire a best friend is the culmination of all the relationship work a child has done up to this point. It began with a secure attachment with parents and continued with parent-directed interactions with peers in play dates, preschool, and other structured interactions. Children next applied these skills when they interacted with peers in elementary school to independently form co-equal relationships. By the time they near the end of the juvenile stage, the hope is that children have learned enough about interacting with others to form a chum relationship, a friendship characterized by trust, responsibility, and love.

MIGUEL AND BROOKS

✳ ✳ ✳

Miguel thinks he looks cool in his new basketball shirt with the name of his favorite player on the back. He admires himself in the mirror and struts around the playground. His best buddy Brooks meets him after school so they can walk home together as they have for the past two years. They walk side by side, looking in store windows and talking about the school day, the teachers, the other kids in class, and what they're going to do this Saturday.

*When they get to Miguel's house, they go up to his
room. As they talk about their favorite basketball players,
Miguel asks Brooks what he thinks about his new basketball
shirt. Brooks says it's okay, but the numbers are too small
and the name on the back isn't really that cool. Miguel
is surprised and asks Brooks again. Brooks repeats his
thoughts. Miguel is upset. He decides to take off the shirt
and put on an old one with another player's name on the
back. They go back to talking and playing.*

A chum's opinion is to be valued and trusted. One terrific
advantage of a chum relationship is that it offers the possibility of
experiencing **consensual validation**. By validation we mean that
what we believe about ourselves or others is shared by someone
we have come to know and trust. Another way to put this is that
because we come to trust our best friend like no one else, his or
her feedback is to be believed. We get a chance to see ourselves
through the eyes of another and, as a result, we obtain information about ourselves that we cannot get anywhere else. Parents
cannot deliver this information because they are not their children's age-mates, or peers. Moreover, parents may not share
their children's values, perspectives, likes, and dislikes.

What can parents do to help children continue to develop
their relationships? We suggest that they facilitate the chum relationship. Even though the time spent with a best friend might
seem excessive, we believe it is essential. Chums help children to
learn who they are and to value another person. In such a relationship, a child learns about himself in ways that are beyond
what parents can teach. Embedded in the chum relationship
is the prototype for long-term, satisfying adult relationships—
relationships in which there is trust, responsibility, and love.

Establishing a healthy sense of control

We've come to the end of a long journey of discovery. Learning to begin, deepen, and end relationships successfully is a major goal of elementary-school-age youngsters, and of all the skills needed to accomplish this goal none is more important than understanding the impact their own behavior has on what happens to them. As you remember, we called this way of looking at the world developing an appropriate level of internal control. In chapter 1, we described *locus of control* as referring to how much of a connection you see between what you do and what happens to you. If you generally see a connection between your actions and outcomes you are **internally controlled**. But if you don't see such connections and instead believe that what happens to you is more the result of luck, fate, chance, or other people, then you are **externally controlled**. A hallmark of successful cognitive and social development in children is becoming more internally controlled with age. The most significant change in locus of control toward internality occurs during the juvenile stage of development as children learn to be independent contributors to the shaping of their lives.

Internal control in children is associated with a variety of positive outcomes. In summary, research shows that internals (compared to externals, their opposites) are more likely to do the following:
- search more actively around them for information that will help them solve their problems and reach their goals
- remember helpful information and use it better
- learn more intentionally and incidentally
- engage in achievement activities more spontaneously
- select more challenging tasks

- delay gratification better
- persist longer at tasks even when they are difficult
- achieve higher levels academically and vocationally
- make more attempts to prevent and remediate their health problems
- maintain better interpersonal relationships
- be more respected and liked by others
- be more resistant to being influenced by others
- have better emotional adjustment as indicated by higher self-esteem, better sense of humor, less anxiety, less depression, and greater satisfaction and contentment with life

This collection of positive outcomes describes a better, more fruitful life for children growing up internal and positions them to learn the skills necessary for interacting successfully.

Parents are the first to help children learn the extent to which their behavior determines what happens to them. Simply put, from the day their children are born parents teach internality through the application of consequences. ("If you eat your vegetables you will get dessert.") Each application teaches children valuable lessons about how they behave and what they can expect from their behavior. Parents who don't apply this model or who apply the model inconsistently are teaching their children to be externally controlled.

For example, if within the family no matter what the child does, something bad happens to her (and, ironically, if no matter what she does, something good happens) then she will develop an external way of looking at the world. Her behavior doesn't matter, so she learns to believe she can do whatever she wants. This view will not serve her well in the world outside of the family where reactions of others are not so predictable.

Children are also taught internality and externality by other adults, especially when they go to school. Teachers and coaches help children learn that their behaviors have consequences. And as children spend more time with peers, they continue learning about behavior and consequences in ways that may be different from what they have previously learned in the home. If you hit another child, chances are that child will hit you back. If you are nice to another child, you can expect them to be nice to you. Children are learning these kinds of contingencies more and more on their own as they spend time with their peers. Because children spend the majority of their days in school it can be a very important learning environment, not only for reading, writing, and arithmetic, but for social interaction as well.

But parents are very important in getting children off to the correct start in learning about locus of control. Research findings from thousands of children demonstrate that parents have a significant impact on the development of locus of control in the home. The general conclusion of the findings is that internality is associated with the following family traits:

- child centeredness and nonauthoritarian child-rearing attitudes in the parents
- a secure home environment
- a strong interest in education
- integrated family activities occur regularly

Elementary-school-age children still have many relationship battles to fight as adolescence approaches. But armed with the knowledge of the way that relationships work and with the nonverbal and verbal skills to communicate how they feel and to pick up the emotions of others, children are well equipped to operate in the interpersonal world. Now they are at a point of development where they can build on their belief that their own actions can govern their relationships and have achieved a sense of the degree to which they can control what happens to them in a broader context. As we have suggested earlier, this belief about their own agency, called an internal locus of control, is a quality that transcends relationships and affects all other important aspects of life.

What is to be accomplished by the end of the juvenile stage?

- to have friends
- to understand others' viewpoints as well as your own
- to understand that much of what happens to you is under your control

CONCLUSION

We began our introduction by saying, "Beyond hearing that a child is doing well in school, few things make a parent's heart leap more for joy than to hear that a child 'has friends'." Our book has been all about making that dream come true. We emphasized four things that are important in your quest to help start your kids out right.

First, developing a secure attachment relationship with your children is essential because it is the structure through which you will teach them the basic skills of relating to others. Second, non-verbal communication, a key element in developing good relationship skills, can be taught and must be learned if children are to build friendships. Third, children who have a strong sense of how their behavior controls what happens to them are more likely to excel at relating. And fourth, parents and teachers must continue to teach and model good relationship behaviors throughout the various stages of development so that their children will grow up with the confidence and the ability to begin and deepen relationships as adolescents and as adults.

The process of acquiring relationship skills begins when a child first forms an attachment relationship with a parent. It is in this special first relationship that children learn their earliest, and perhaps their most important, lessons about relating to others. We described what parents must provide for their children so they can form a healthy, secure attachment relationship, a bond that gives children the self-confidence and trust in others they need in order to begin making friends.

One of the significant truths about relationships is that they are built on the foundation of both verbal and nonverbal social language. We emphasize the importance of the nonverbal because it is often overlooked after children leave infancy and begin to use words to communicate with others. Nonverbal communication skills should not be neglected in childhood and adolescence, because nonverbal communication remains important for relationship development throughout a person's life.

Almost from the very beginning of life, children seem to want to act on their environment to control it. Learning to perceive the appropriate connection between your actions and what happens to you—becoming internally controlled—is one of the most important goals of childhood. Why is this so important? One answer is that internally controlled individuals approach all problems, especially those presented by relationships, with the idea that their efforts will make a difference. This is a healthy attitude that results in greater relationship success.

We believe that the ability to relate well to others consists, in large measure, of learned skills. And while children learn certain relationship skills from experiences with their peers, many of their earliest and most lasting relationship lessons come from listening to and watching the adults in their lives relate to others. This means that parents and teachers have a terrific opportunity to impart valuable lessons about relationships to their children. Children whose parents and teachers have modeled, taught, and reinforced effective ways to relate to others are more likely to have the confidence and ability to develop successful relationships as adolescents and adults.

All parents have a chance to start their kids off right. The task begins, very simply, with understanding the important role you as a parent play in your interactions with your children, whether they are three months, three years, or thirteen years old. It continues, despite the busyness of your lives, as you make a little time every day to bring your conscious awareness and your full presence to your interactions with your kids. And it means knowing that your children need you as a role model, cheerleader, and guide (and sometimes patient observer) as they begin to venture forth and develop their own friendships.

Each phase of a child's growth, from infancy to childhood to the juvenile stage, has its distinctive joys, but also its daunting challenges. Time demands, our own fears, the temperament of our children, and a million other things can short-circuit our attempts to provide what we know our children need to become relationship savvy. For example, infants, toddlers, and children are not always receptive to feedback that tells them that there are better ways to behave. Sometimes our own tendency to overreact makes us say things to our kids that are less than helpful. And we are not always ready to let our children move away from us to experience the wider world and its unpredictability. Raising children is an extremely difficult and humbling experience!

But we believe that these challenges can be successfully negotiated. All children will face difficulties. Some children will have more problems than others. That's where you as parents come in: teaching and modeling relationship skills, providing opportunities for children to relate to others, encouraging them, praising their successes, and supporting them in myriad other ways. With persistence, patience, and a willingness to take things "one day at time" you can help children overcome these difficulties.

Keep in mind that it takes time to develop good habits. This is just as true for learning good relationship skills as it is for acquiring any other habit. It's important that we're patient with ourselves and with our kids as they develop competence in relating to other people. Remember, also, that there is no such thing as perfection when it comes to relationships and that it is through mistakes and missteps that kids learn. Learning about relationships is a lifelong process. The best way to set the stage for our kids to have rewarding relationships throughout their lives is to model and encourage openness and interest in others, a willingness to learn from experience, and a sense of joy and optimism about the process.

Because teaching about relationships is such an important and demanding part of parenting, we urge you to ask for help when you encounter problems. Talk to others. You will find that you have lots of allies—teachers, family physicians, other family members, your own close friends, rabbis and ministers, counselors—who can offer you insights and encouragement. Throughout the book we've given you the names of a number of leading experts on relationships, and at the end of the book we provide you a variety of ways to gather more information about all sorts of social interaction. And we encourage you to e-mail us to share your stories of frustration and success (snowick@emory.edu; psymd@emory.edu).

We've presented both a set of practical techniques for teaching children relationship skills and a larger vision of the possibilities that successful relationships offer for your child. Our observations come not only from our experiences as parents and professionals, but also from our own and others' research.

Why is all this all so important? It is because you are preparing your child for developing strong and happy future relationships.

We stopped the discussion at preadolescence, when children are poised on the brink of their journey into adulthood. When parents have done their job properly up to that stage, their children will have the tools they need to grapple with the problems seen and unseen yet to come.

Melissa Fay Greene, award-winning author, has written that "The difference between no friends and two good friends is like the difference between a pitch-black room and one lit by birthday candles." We could not agree more. Helping children learn how to relate is a long, hard process, but the effort is worth it. Children who learn how to make friends and be friends in childhood are more likely to grow up to be adults who make good, happy, and meaningful lives for themselves. This is what we wish for all children.

Selected Bibliography

Biddulph, Steve. *The Secret of Happy Children: Why Children Behave the Way They Do—and What You Can Do to Help Them to Be Optimistic, Loving, Capable and Happy.* Marlowe & Co., 2002.

Crouter, Ann C., and Alan Booth, eds. *Children's Influence on Family Dynamics: The Neglected Side of Family Relationships* (Penn State University Family Issues Symposia). Lawrence Erlbaum, 2003.

Duke, Marshall, Nowicki, Stephen, and Elisabeth Martin. *Teaching Your Child the Language of Social Success.* Peachtree Publishers, 1996.

Faber, Adele, and Elaine Mazlish. *How To Talk So Kids Will Listen and Listen So Kids Will Talk.* Collins, 1999.

Fulghum, Robert. *From Beginning to End: the Rituals of Our Lives.* Fawcett, 1996.

Galinsky, Ellen, and Judy David. *The Preschool Years: Family Strategies That Work—From Experts and Parents.* Ballantine, 1990.

Glenn, H. Stephen, and Jane Nelsen. *Raising Self-Reliant Children in a Self-Indulgent World: Seven Building Blocks for Developing Capable Young People.* Prima, 2000.

Goleman, Daniel. *Emotional Intelligence: Why It Can Matter More Than IQ.* Bantam, 2005.

————. *Social Intelligence: The New Science of Human Relationships.* Bantam, 2007.

Gottman, John, and Joan Declaire. *Raising an Emotionally Intelligent Child.* Simon & Schuster, 1998.

Hall, Nadia, Kulkarni, Chaya, and Shauna Seneca. *Your Guide to Nurturing Parent-Child Relationships: Positive Parenting Activities for Home Visitors.* Paul H. Brookes, 2007.

Kabat-Zinn, Jon, and Myla Kabat-Zinn. *Everyday Blessings.* Hyperion, 1997.

Lerner, Harriet. *The Mother Dance: How Children Change Your Life.* HarperCollins, 1998.

Murray, Bob, and Alicia Fortinbery. *Raising an Optimistic Child: A Proven Plan for Depression-Proofing Young Children—For Life.* McGraw-Hill, 2005.

Nelsen, Jane. *Positive Discipline.* Ballantine. 2006.

Nowicki, Stephen, and Marshall Duke. *Helping the Child Who Doesn't Fit In.* Peachtree Publishers, 1992.

Osman, Betty. *No One to Play With: Social Problems of LD and ADD Children.* Academic Therapy Publications, 1989.

Pianta, Robert C. *Enhancing Relationships Between Children and Teachers.* American Psychological Association, 1999.

Rosenfeld, Alvin, Wise, Nicole, and Robert Coles. *The Over-Scheduled Child: Avoiding the Hyper-Parenting Trap.* St. Martin's Griffin, 2001.

Seligman, Martin. *The Optimistic Child: A Proven Program to Safeguard Children Against Depression and Build Lifelong Resilience.* Houghton Mifflin, 2007.

Siegel, Daniel, and Mary Hartzell. *Parenting from the Inside Out: How a Deeper Self-Understanding Can Help You Raise Children Who Thrive.* Tarcher/Penguin, 2004.

Sunderland, Margot. *The Science of Parenting: How Today's Brain Research Can Help You Raise Happy, Emotionally Balanced Children.* DK, 2008.

Taffel, Ron. *Parenting By Heart: How to Stay Connected to Your Child in a Disconnected World.* Perseus, 2002.

Acknowledgments

We would like to thank all the parents and children with whom we have related over all these past years. They have provided us with unending knowledge and wisdom concerning what makes life worth living, that is, connecting with one another.

The book never would have come into existence without the help, guidance, and support of the Peachtree Publishers family. Margaret Quinlin, who has been with us from the very beginning of our publishing life, and Vicky Holifield, who has patiently turned our ideas into intelligible prose, we are grateful for your expertise but more so for your friendship. Thank you.

The ideas presented in this book are build on a strong foundation of research that has been ongoing for nearly four decades. We wish to thank all those students and colleagues who have contributed to what we know about relationships. Without their help and information we could not have applied our ideas practically to the lives of children and their parents.

Lastly we thank our own parents and our own children and grandchildren whose lives have constantly reminded us that there is nothing in this world more important than relationships. Each of us would not have enjoyed the riches of parenthood without our spouses. To Kaaren, Sara, and John we offer our thanks and our everlasting love for the support they have given us through the completion of this book and for making life so worth living.

Index

About the Authors

MARSHALL P. DUKE, PhD, holds degrees from Rutgers University and Indiana University. He is Charles Howard Candler Professor of Personality and Psychopathology at Emory University. Duke was the cowinner of the Applied Researchers of the Year Award from the American Psychological Association. He has published numerous scholarly articles and coauthored several books, including HELPING THE CHILD WHO DOESN'T FIT IN, TEACHING YOUR CHILD THE LANGUAGE OF SOCIAL SUCCESS, and WHAT WORKS WITH CHILDREN. He lives in Georgia.

STEPHEN NOWICKI JR., PhD, received his PhD from Purdue University. He is Charles Howard Candler Professor of Psychology at Emory University. Nowicki was the cowinner of the Applied Researchers of the Year Award from the American Psychological Association. He is the author of numerous publications and presentations and the coauthor of several books, including HELPING THE CHILD WHO DOESN'T FIT IN and TEACHING YOUR CHILD THE LANGUAGE OF SOCIAL SUCCESS. He lives in Georgia.

AMY VAN BUREN, PhD, received her BA in English from Williams College and her doctorate in clinical psychology from Emory University. She is an Associate Professor of Psychology at Sacred Heart University in Fairfield, Connecticut. She has published articles on nonverbal behavior, attachment in adults and children, and interpersonal relationships. In addition to teaching at Sacred Heart, she gives frequent public lectures on topics ranging from parenting to emotional intelligence to the psychology of everyday adjustment. She lives in Connecticut with her husband and son.

Northport-East Northport Public Library

MAY 2009

To view your patron record from a computer, click on the Library's homepage: **www.nenpl.org**

You may:
- request an item be placed on hold
- renew an item that is overdue
- view titles and due dates checked out on your card
- view your own outstanding fines

**151 Laurel Avenue
Northport, NY 11768
631-261-6930**